OUT OF CONTROL

From Darkness to Light & Love!

JEFFREY A. LIND

OUT OF CONTROL
© Copyright 2021 — Jeffrey A. Lind

All rights reserved. This book is protected under the copyright laws of the United States. No part of this publication may be reproduced, stored in a retrieval system or transmitted in any form or by any means, including electronic, mechanical, photocopying, recording or otherwise, without the prior written permission of the copyright owner, except by a reviewer, who may quote brief passages in a review.

This book may not be copied or reprinted for commercial gain or profit. The use of short quotations is permitted and encouraged.

Design by NorthStarVoice.net

ISBN : 978-1-73-673747-7

For worldwide distribution. Printed in the United States.

CONTENTS

References

Acknowledgment

About the Author

Dear Reader

Controlling All   15

Hidden Life to Maintain Control   21

Anger, the Evil Monster Within   25

Needing No One   33

Gravitating to Others   41

Escaping Commitment with Biblical Reasoning   49

Dying Slowly Within   55

Medical Issues and Death   59

Your Eternal Light   67

Loving Me for Who I Am and Knowing Who I Am   75

Investing in Faith, Prayer, and Donning My Armor   81

Foundation of God's Word and in Your Marriage   93

Eternally and Happily Married Forever After   107

A Little Extra Love

REFERENCES

Unless otherwise indicated, all scripture are from the *New King James Version* NKJV www.biblestudytolls.com/nkjv commissioned in 1975 by Thomas Nelson Publishers. All rights reserved.

Verses marked NIV are taken from the *New International Version Bible*, www.biblestudytools.com commissioned in 1967, the New York Bible Society (noe Biblica) generously created a contemporary English translation of the Bible.

Verses marked KJV are taken from the *King James Version of the Bible*. The King James Study Bible (previously published as The Liberty Annotated Study Bible and as The Annotated Study Bible, King James Version) Copyright 1988 by Liberty University.

Verses marked ESV are from *The English Standard Version* (ESV) which is an essentially literal translation of the Bible in contemporary English. Created by a team of more than 100 leading evangelical scholars and pastors, www.esv.org, as the ESV Bible emphasizes word-for-word accuracy, literary excellence, and depth of meaning.

Fireproof is a 2008 American Christian drama film released by Samuel Goldwyn Films and Affirm Films, directed by Alex Kendrick, who co-wrote and co-produced it with Stephen Kendrick. The film stars Kirk Cameron, Erin Bethea, and Ken Bevel.

Fireproof Your Marriage: Participant's Guide, 2008, Jennifer Dion, 097871539X, 9780978715397, Daywind, 2008.

The Five Love Languages (1992) — Written by Dr. Gary Chapman, and "The Five Languages of Apology" (2016) — Written by Dr. Gary Chapman with Jennifer Thomas.

Quotes and Teachings by Dr. Louis and Pastor Tina Kayatin.

A Love Worth Fighting For Marriage Event (2017) — Kirk Cameron and www.marriagemissions.com by Marriage Missions International.

Quotes by Yehuda Berg — *Words*

Quotes by Dave Willis — *When I'm Worried*

Quote by the late Glen Ball — *A Ready Word*

Key Elements of Successful Communication Pie Chart (1967) — Albert Mehrabian

House Building Principles — Out of Zion Counseling Ministry at Christ is King Vineyard Church and education provided by Rev. David S. Weiss, M.A.

Definitions by Wikipedia, The Free Encyclopedia. Wikipedia is hosted by the Wikimedia Foundation, a non-profit organization that also hosts a range of other projects. The Creative Commons Attribution ShareAlike License.

Every effort has been made to give proper credit for all stories, educational material, quotes, poems, and quotations. If for any reason proper credit has not been given, please notify the author and/or publisher and proper notation with be given on future printings.

ACKNOWLEDGEMENT

I would like to thank my dear, sweet and loving wife, Shawn C. Lind, for your assistance, guidance, patience, suggestions, and loving encouragement on this project.

DEDICATION

This book is dedicated to Shawn's (My) parents Jack and LaDonna Burks whom passed into the arms of our Loving Savior Jesus Christ just prior to the first publishing of this book. We will always remember, honor, and cherish the memories, opportunities, and experiences we had with them along the way.

I will always Thank them for Loving me as if I were their own son and for Always showing us how to live life to the fullest and Loving Everyone along the way!

ABOUT THE AUTHOR

Jeffrey Allen Lind is a man that has gone through various everyday trials and struggles of marriage and life. He is a veteran of The U.S. Army and USARNG. He is Married to Shawn Crystal Lind, the father of 4 adult children, and a Grandfather. He enjoys the outdoors, four-wheeling, and especially playing in the sand and sea when able to go snorkeling and scuba diving. He prefers to be spending quality time with his family and out adventuring throughout God's country with his wonderful wife. He also loves to watch college football in his spare time. He is a practicing Christian and loves to spread the good news of God's Love, Life and Light to ALL. He chooses to shine a new light on the Covenant of Marriage, and the amazing benefits that a exemplary Life of Love and Loving God First will bring to your marriage.

DEAR READER

Dear Reader,

We are pleased that you have chosen to read this book and invest in your marriage. This book is a real-life testimony of God's Grace, Mercy, and Love. It is a story of His never-ending Love which has allowed for personal healing, forgiveness, saving our marriage, and allowing these words to Proclaim His Glory to Everyone. Several years in the making, this book has been a labor of Love and conviction to spreads God's message to all who will receive it. We pray that everyone will receive the messages and teachings within, with an open mind and heart. Also allowing for oneness, to be able to give their life to God, and becoming the best spouse that they can be in the Name of Our Father God Almighty. This book was written with the intent of assisting our adult children in their marriages and any other couples looking to truly be inspired along the way. To allow others to see the life and journey that we have endured and overcame by the Grace of God.

We started our lives together without even considering God as a part of our daily lives, throughout our dating relationship, or even during the first several years of our ensuing marriage. Be like the wise man and not the fool as we once were! "Everyone then who hears these words of mine and does them will be like a wise man who built his house on the rock. And the rain fell, and the floods came, and the wind blew, and beat on the house, but it did not fall, because it had been founded on the rock. And everyone who hears these words of mine and does not do them and will be like a foolish man who built his house of the sand. And then rain fell, and the floods came, and then wind blew and beat against the house, and it fell, and great was the fall of it." Matthew 7:24-27, ESV

Now that our marriage has been surrendered to God to do His perfect will and perfect way individually, He has rescued, revitalized, renewed, rekindled, and refreshed our marriage in the Name of Jesus! It has been a battle for almost 19 years of our marriage, and we know that we still need to continue to fight for our marriage every day in today's ever-changing world. We've committed our lives and our marriage to God, continuing to pray over our marriage. We continuously pray over all marriages between husband and wife to also succeed Faithfully and Flourish in His Mighty Name. And for all married couples to see a glimpse of God's Love & Light for their marriages. We Boldly pray circles around ALL marriages, including our children's marriages, the generations to come, and our very own marriage. We pray just like the Israelites marched around Jericho. We pray in faith that God will reveal Himself to heal those marriages that read this book and turn their hearts to Him to fight the Good fight of Faith. We pray over all marriages, Ezekiel 36:26, "I will give you a new heart and put a new spirit in you; I will remove from you your heart of stone and give you a heart of Flesh." NIV

Accordingly, we as sons and daughters of God must do our part and get up every morning to put on the full armor of God. Ephesians 6:11-18, "Put on the whole armor of God, that you may be able to stand against the wiles of the devil. For we do not wrestle against flesh and blood, but against principalities, against powers, against the ruler of the darkness of this age, against spiritual hosts of wickedness in the heavenly places. Therefore take up the whole armor of God, that you may be able to withstand in the evil day, and having done all to stand. Stand therefore, having girded your waist with truth, having put on the breastplate of righteousness, and having shod your feet with the preparation of the gospel of peace: above all, taking the shield of faith with which you will be able to quench all the fiery darts of the wicked one. And take the helmet of salvation, and the sword of the Spirit, which is the word of God; praying always with all prayer and supplication in the Spirit, being watchful to this end with all perseverance and supplication of all the saints."

A great young pastor once told his congregation on a Sunday morning, "no one asked David to go fight Goliath, he just knew that it was his calling. David donned his armor, asked God for His blessing and provision before he would ever stand before the mighty Philistine. Then stepped outside of the boundaries that once labeled him just a shepherd boy, prayed audaciously and undoubtedly, and then went out and conquered a giant in the name of God."

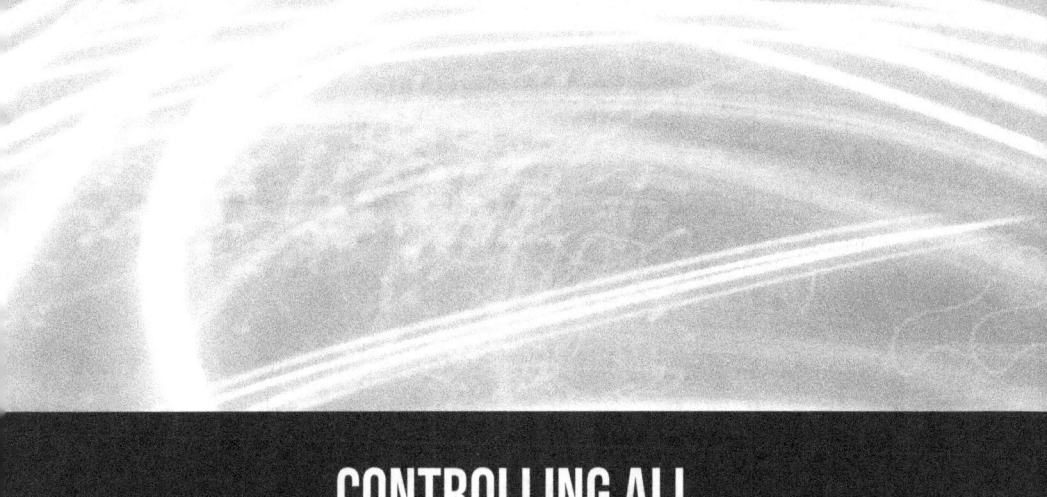

CONTROLLING ALL

It always amazes me to see the Glory of God in my life when He knows all the things I've done wrong, but that proves how awesome of a God He is toward us. Even when we don't feel worthy, He always deems us worthy. I can't stop the tears from flowing when I know how much He loves me each day, and gives me new opportunities to love Him back. This is a love story far greater than any other love I've ever felt. It saved my life and our marriage for all eternity.

I am your ordinary man that thought if I wanted to get ahead in life, I needed to take the bull by the horns. I had to make things happen for myself — no matter what the cost, whether relationally or in monetary value. Carpe Diem (Seize the Day) was what I was taught in the U.S. Army. You want something, you go after it, right? You have to put all your thoughts, emotions, and ambitions into making your dreams come true.

I was married, had three children (Andrew, Aaron, and Alyssa), a dog, a house, several cars, lots of friends, and more. I felt I was living the

All-American dream. At least that was my take on life growing up and becoming a man. I was going to make everything perfect and there was nothing that could change any of that.

Then one day that all diminished in a heartbeat. My wife of nine+ years decided to leave. We eventually divorced. The courts decided to place our children with their mother. They were only allowing me to have weekend and summer visitations, and that's how it would remain for the next two years.

Feeling unfit as a parent, I turned to partying and drinking alcohol excessively. I attempted wild and crazy feats. I was trying desperately to move on in my relationship, including a failed engagement that lasted one month. I was going to make things happen. I would make myself happy.

One night, while out with some friends, I met Shawn. She was a beautiful younger woman that seemed so different from any other woman I have met. Intrigued, I asked her to go on several dates. She agreed. She, too, was curious about who I was. She was interested in my life, my children, my family, and my friends. She had a son (Erik) who was six. She felt like a wonderful, different fit for my life.

We continued dating, having our ups and downs with four children. We then lived together for two years. She eventually agreed to marry me on August 24, 2002.

This all came about after I badgered her. She communicated her best intentions for us to please consider waiting. She was going from only her son being with her full time to then having two summers and every other weekend with four kids. And now a full-fledged family of six. And if I could only get her to agree, we would soon be a family of seven. What can I say? I like children! And I was going to again make everything "Great" in my life!

I knew that I had a great job and we loved each other. So what could be better than all of that? We moved closer to my job and away from our families, which would make things even better for us. Then we didn't have to hear the daily influences of our parents or anyone else who wanted to give their opinions that didn't matter to me. I would take care of my family the way that I wanted to take care of my family. Nothing was going to stop me this time from that perfect dream of living happily ever after. I mean why not? I am a hopeless romantic and my dreams were going to finally come true.

I had a beautiful wife, a job making bank, four great children, a wonderful chocolate Lab named Fudge. I drove a brand new Chevy Trailblazer EXT. The only thing left was to get a house for our new family.

We met this amazing couple who owned our eventual house, and we immediately fell in love with them and the house. Bobby and Greg are such amazing people. Warm, inviting, genuine, sincere ... and it felt like we had known them for years in what was only a few hours.

But there was one stipulation — we must attend their church one time and give it a try. So we agreed and I bought Shawn the biggest, best house my money could buy. I knew there was no way she couldn't be happy on 2.2 acres outside of town but close to work and new work friends. We were doing what we thought was best for our family.

Now don't get me wrong, it is what we wanted to do. But it was more of what I wanted and, again, I was going to make this happen. So we did go to Church on the North Coast in Lorain, Ohio as we promised we would. We went back whenever we felt the urge over the next year. We knew that something felt different. It was comfortable, loving, accepting, and right for us. It was just like when we met Bobby and Greg … like something or someone was luring us with this amazing feeling. We weren't getting this feeling in our ordinary everyday life.

One Sunday night while laying in bed with Shawn, we were talking about some different things. I said to her, "You know I was thinking about church and how everyone makes us feel so loved. It feels comfortable." She replied, "You know, that's funny because I was laying here thinking the exact same thing!" It was an amazing moment in our lives. We felt like we were finally taking a step in the right direction, not only for ourselves but for our family as well.

So we concluded that we needed to attend CNC on a regular weekly basis. We always felt loved and accepted for who we were. We felt more accepted by our new church family, friends, and Pastoral staff than other people in our lives. For whatever the reason may have been. It was almost like we were given special interest or increased favor. I could never understand why until years down the road.

So we have continued to attend CNC for that past 14 years and still love it. But something was still amiss in our home. I would dabble in and out of the ways we were taught of being faithful to God and distancing ourselves from the ways of the world, and I continued to have one foot firmly planted in this world. And the other lightly treading on the other side of the cross.

I even remember getting mad at Shawn in our kitchen one day when she mentioned the way I was acting. It was right after we had returned from church. I blew up at her calling her "Holier than Thou." I also remember other arguments over insignificant things. Issues like having hot dogs and baked beans for supper.

One evening I went off on her because I stated that I make better money than this. I work my butt off going in early every morning and staying late each night. I then would come home and have a crappy meal like this. I deserve better!

We continued to fight about raising children, our finances, generic strawberry syrup, what we would do each night because I was bored, sex and what she was wearing to bed, or where we would go for vacations, etc.

I felt, "I work hard, I make amazing money, and I can do whatever I want to do." So she would do her best to appease me. But it was never enough even though we had all we needed and more. What else could I want? We lived in a mansion according to our coworkers. I did whatever I could think of to stay busy. I had a beautiful wife, and four wonderful children to spend time with every other weekend and throughout every summer.

Wrong! I still wasn't satisfied with anything and everything. I wanted and needed more.

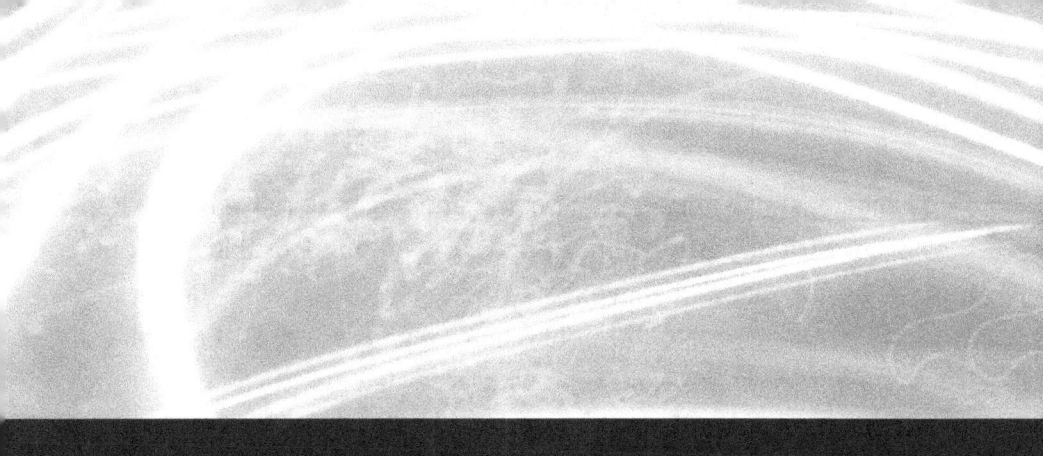

HIDDEN LIFE TO MAINTAIN CONTROL

Since it was up to me to take charge as the breadwinner in this family, I needed to do something different so I could do what I wanted, and make what I wanted to happen when I wanted it to happen.

So one day after another argument about finances, I demanded that I would take over all control of our finances from this point further and that I would be making all of the financial decisions from here on out. That would be the last time that I discussed our financial status or situations with Shawn. And it would be the last time I would eat hot dogs and baked beans for dinner unless I was attending a picnic at one of her family members' houses.

Of course, no one in my family would serve that for dinner even if it was a picnic! It would be Angus burgers with amazing sides like my mother's potato salad (the best) at the very least, if not even grilled chicken, kabobs, and/or steak. Come on now, right!

So I took over the household finances and began to make myself happy again with no reservations of any cost, situation, or anyone's opinion. I did ask, once I believe, what the kids wanted — 4 wheelers for each of us, or an inground pool. Their response was 4 wheelers. But that meant spending more time with my in-laws who had more property than we had and a pole barn to store all of the equipment. This would then mean that we would have to go to their property and be around people that I didn't want to necessarily be around. They lived a different lifestyle than I was trying to promote in my family, and I quite honestly thought that we were better than that.

I formulated this opinion, unfairly based on my upbringing and the new lifestyle that I had desired and deserved. So, I decided that I would buy a $50,000 fiberglass heated inground swimming pool, installed with "all of the bells and whistles that you could ever imagine." I also bought a six person hot tub sunken into our deck for easier access. And, oh yeah, an indoor stand-up tanning booth for my trophy wife so she could always look amazing to me and for me whenever I wanted her to be my prized possession, or when I wanted to take her and show her off at our employer's yearly Christmas drunken bash.

I was in the process of molding and changing all of the little unrefined parts of my wife and my life. I changed the way she spoke, acted, her image (including wearing her hair a certain way or cut to a current new style), and I would even pick out most of the clothing that she wore. I did have a knack for her to look stylish with current trends, but I think that she just went along with it to not cause a ripple in our relationship and to appease me as always.

I would continue to spend, spend, spend until my heart's content. Ultimately, it buried us in mounds of debt. I happily continued to mold, shape, and change my life to match the image that I desired for my life.

But again, this wasn't enough. I could never ever have enough. Whether it was my wife, money, possessions, or time vacationing with my family. Shawn and I went on many vacations to amazing places like the Bahamas, Jamaica, and Cancun just so I could get more of her away from everyone else and see that amazing "trophy wife" body in a bikini. And we would also take multiple family vacations between these personal excursions with our children every year from Florida (including Disney and Busch Gardens), to Daytona and Michigan (to famous race tracks), and wherever else I could think of going in-between to buy everyone's affection.

For some reason, I thought that I needed to do all of this and that it would make me happier since I knew I was making all of them happy.

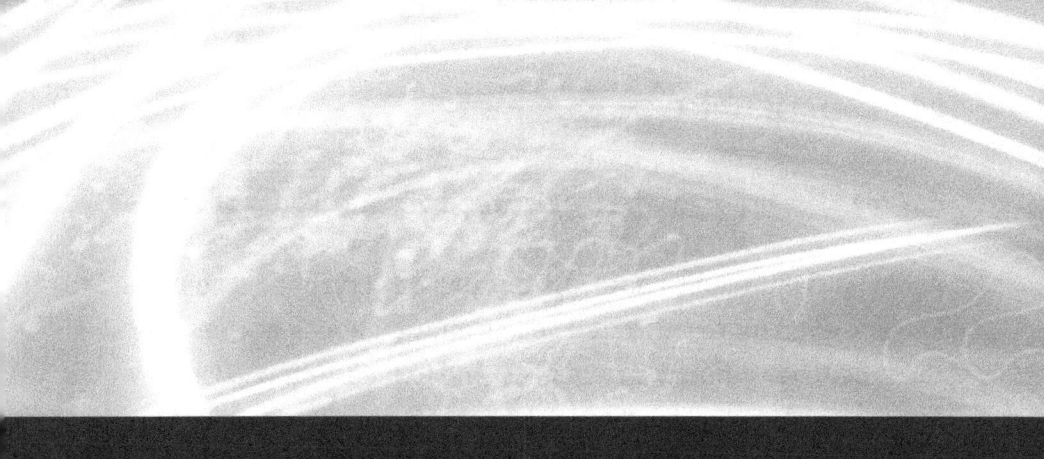

ANGER, THE EVIL MONSTER WITHIN

Well, I guess selfishness and pride definitely got in my way throughout this portion of my life and through the first 5-6 years of our marriage as well.

So, I came to the conclusion that money and possessions weren't going to buy me enough happiness in my life. I had everything, more than anyone could possibly want and/or need, and I still wasn't happy with the route that my life was going. Since I still wasn't happy with all of these possessions in my life, I became bitter, angry, and frustrated at everyone and everything. I was even angry with God whom I knew (or thought I knew). I thought I understood God since I was going to church regularly.

I heard His word every week and I prayed for things to change with my wife, my children, our relationships, my work situations, and especially my lack of happiness of life. The major problem with this was, my "stinking thinking!" I would pray for things that I wanted, not situations or circumstances that came into agreement with God's plans for me, my wife, us, or for the greater good of our children's lives.

As things continued to not work out the way I planned, I continued to become even more frustrated yelling and screaming at everyone all of the time. Then when they would ask me to please stop yelling, I would say, "You call this yelling, I'll let you hear what yelling sounds like," and become increasingly louder and more obnoxious. I also became very demanding all of the time to have my way and to do what I wanted when I wanted. And now!

I became somewhat of a drill sergeant to my children and even more of an idiot toward my wife. I would tell my children, "I don't care what you want or what you want to do. You do as I say, when I say. This is Rome and I'm the Emperor!" I also would continuously treat Shawn like crap and demand that things would happen in certain ways, including things she didn't want to do or felt very uncomfortable doing, whether it was dressing a certain way or wearing certain things to bed to satisfy my every desire.

As more time passed, the more I continued to control everyone and every situation the way I wanted. If it didn't happen immediately, I became even more unsatisfied and angry. So when the people in my life couldn't meet my expectations and make me happy anymore, I turned to the world of pornography, videoing, and trying to recreate these images into real-life situations with my wife in the bedroom.

There wasn't anything that I didn't want from her or didn't expect her to comply with since she was my wife and that's what wives are supposed to do — satisfy their husbands. As I heard in church, "Wives, submit yourselves to your own husbands."

Hold on ladies! Before you crucify me, obviously, this was outside of the correct context. But that's what I heard, thought, and felt at this point in my life. And of course, it was all about me being happy. I had become this increasingly angry, self-centered, egotistical, aggressive, and pathetic Monster.

Shawn would then become even more afraid of these situations in our lives and threaten to leave without returning. So, I would apologize as I always did after the fact to make everything alright again, at least in my head, and tell her that I would never do any of it again.

But I would beg for mercy from her in one breath and just do it again the next time. Shawn has told me since I started writing this book that she would even say these same apologies in her head as I was saying them aloud because she had already heard it 100,000 times before.

As I continued to live this endless cycle at home, it started to flow over into my work life with people beginning to see that I wasn't satisfied with the lifestyle and especially the relationship that Shawn and I had. As I started confiding in "friends," I started hearing about alternative lifestyles and people coming into agreement with me that this is not what life is all about. They said my family and wife should be more in tune with my way of thinking and that wives are supposed to keep their husbands satisfied, and that's the number one reason why people step outside of their respective marriages or try alternative measures to spice up their relationships.

The more I confided in my coworkers the more I was becoming increasingly convinced that I deserved more from Shawn, and deserved a better lifestyle all the way around. I then would try to make Shawn feel guilty for not providing for her husband's needs, wants, and desires. I would tell her why don't you just divorce me since you don't want to do the things that a wife is supposed to do. I would say there are a lot of other women out there who would absolutely love to have a husband like me, her lifestyle, and all of the things that came with it. A husband that spoils her while living in a mansion, does household chores without being asked, and works hard to bring home a steady paycheck to live to the standards that we were living.

I would hear from younger women at work that Shawn was very lucky to have me and that they would love to have a guy like me that provided such an amazing lifestyle for her. Or they would ask if I had a brother like me so they, too, could have a "Sugar Daddy" type of lifestyle.

Then I would work longer hours each night and weekends to just see and spend time with one particular woman, and converse even more with these other women to feed my desires. And besides, I was making even more money working overtime to maintain the lifestyle that I had created. Win, Win!

So I continued to live with this mentality and trying things to spice up my love life using pornography as a tool to satisfy my desires in the bedroom with my wife. But the more I tried these things, the more Shawn became distant to me and any type of lifestyle like this. I then started talking to those younger, promiscuous women more frequently at work to test the waters. I also talked to women on the internet on adult websites.

And as the old adage goes among guys, "Nothing wrong with getting your appetite somewhere else as long as you eat at home." I would even set up potential meetings with these women but never went through with it.

But then, it happened. A mutual friend of ours that was like her best friend was around quite often and she was younger and single, so I decided to take the opportunity to go to her apartment one afternoon when Shawn thought that I was still working. I propositioned her friend and tried to paint this wonderful picture of romance and sex.

Nothing actually happened between us because she had more morals than I and couldn't do that to her friend, my wife. When Shawn found out, we began to argue even more about our relationship or lack thereof and where we were headed — straight to the world of separation. I attempted to cross a barrier that should've been off-limits from the beginning of our marriage. It should not have even been in my feeble mind.

She came back after several months of being apart, and we went to counseling but things never changed. She, again and again, threatened to leave for good and never return. But again I pleaded my case and for mercy, saying that I could change. I said that I would get help with my pornography addiction, and we could go to more Christian couples counseling. But I really only continued to manipulate every situation to make it look so promising and scent it with a smell of Roses and hope for us.

To be perfectly honest though, these were just selfish motives to have my cake and eat it too. I really had no intention of changing anything, but I would continue going through the motions and continued through the same never-ending cycle.

While all of this continued to go on, I always felt that there was something in the back of my mind, something that I could never truly understand or put my finger on. Something that I thought I knew, but could never make happen. This was to be able to live the lifestyle of other God-fearing couples that I would see every Sunday at CNC. A God-fearing life with Him being enough, and being more in me than me in this world.

But this back and forth battle ensued for the next 2-3 years of my life, even though I continued to hear chapter after chapter of the Bible flowing like a refreshing river every Sunday in church. Versus like:

Exodus 20:14: "You shall not commit adultery."

Matthew 5:28: "But I tell you that anyone who looks at a woman lustfully has already committed adultery with her in his heart."

2 Timothy 2:22: "Flee the evil desires of youth and pursue righteousness, faith, love, and peace, along with those who call on the Lord of a pure heart."

1 John 2:16: "For everything in the world — the lust of the flesh, the lust of the eyes, and the pride of life — comes not from the Father but from the world."

These verses would fill the atmosphere and enter my mind, but still, I just could not grasp the concept of the things that I was doing wrong. I could not see what God really wanted me to envision. It was like I was single-minded with blinders on for only my way of thinking and how I wanted my life.

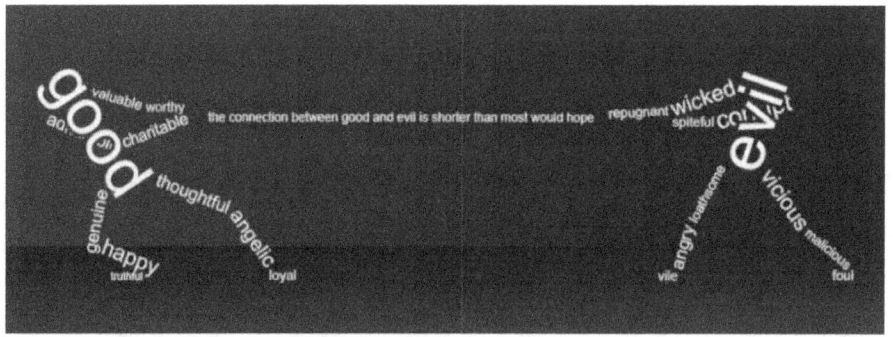

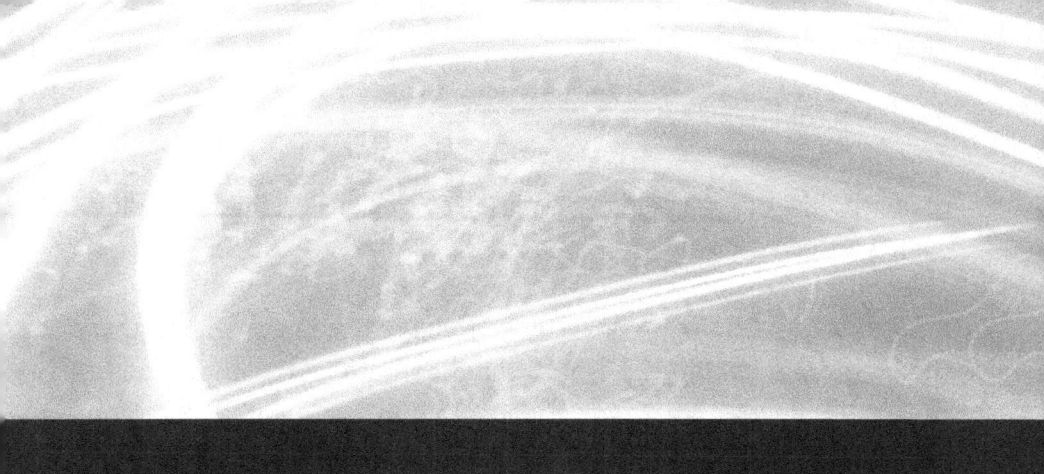

NEEDING NO ONE

Even though I would try to do better, or tried to make things right with God, for myself and everyone around me, I just could not accomplish this daunting task. So, I just gave up. I truly had enough; I just couldn't do it anymore. I was totally and completely done. So, I thought about things for a while and decided that this is not what I wanted for my life, my wife, or our marriage, or for my children to continue this never-ending cycle of heartbreak, distress, and anger.

I thought about every possible way of getting out of my marriage, for my life situations to just vanish, or better yet, for me to just permanently be gone. So, while giving up on everything and everyone, I then fell into this endless cycle of sickness and battling my every inner thought. I didn't even want to get out of bed each morning to go to work.

My days at work were long and miserable and my days at home were even longer because I would just sit at home and battle my dismal inner thoughts. I then began to make myself ill with my thoughts which I believed started causing migraine headaches, vomiting, lightheadedness, photophobia, etc., I would make myself so sick on certain days, I didn't even want to survive.

I began to ask God to remove these things, these people, and these thoughts from my life. Everyone would be better off without me because all I did was create misery and pain in everyone's life. No one truly ever understood me and no one ever could or would. All I ever wanted was to truly be loved, accepted for who I am, that I wasn't a bad person. And that I was a loveable person too.

I only did the things of the past to try to make everyone happy, including myself. But the more I prayed in this solemn isolated place I had created in my life, God never answered, and the more I withdrew.

I didn't want to be around anyone or anything. I wouldn't go to work, church, family gatherings, or even my children's sporting events. I enjoyed being left alone and having others feel sorry for me because my world was a complete role reversal. I once was at the top of my game making big money and loving every minute of it. Or so people thought. And these same people who saw me as this awesome guy, husband, coworker, conquering all, now saw me as a victim of circumstances and situations and that I had no control over.

But what I found out was that not one of those people that thought I was the greatest husband, father, coworker, employee, the guy they wanted to be with, or friend were ever there for me when I delved into this lonely dark place. I didn't even think that God really cared about me either because he didn't help me deal with any of my problems. And He definitely didn't take me out of my misery as I would lay there many days and nights curled in a fetal position on my bed in the total darkness of our room.

I begged and pleaded for Him to just not allow me to wake up and deal with this lack of life that I was struggling with each day. Shawn and I continued to have our usual fights and new battles because of my lack of desire to do anything or be around anyone. I didn't want to work, and our finances were now suffering because I continued to spend all of my time putting us in debt. And now we couldn't afford to pay for basic necessities and were always behind in paying our bills. We couldn't even really afford to put food on our table at times after the house payment on that mansion of a house, plus all of the other expenses that went into upkeep and maintenance.

We would continue to fight and argue almost daily when I wasn't sick about all of the money issues we were having and that I had adopted this "I don't care mentality" about everyone or everything. Shawn would leave and come back and leave again every time we fought but I didn't even care about that anymore either. I would just throw it in her face that she never loved me and was always just running away to mommy and daddy to solve her problems as she always did because she couldn't handle real life. But in fact, I would just continue to re-insure my "stinking thinking" by saying to myself, and sometimes out loud to her, that she never really loved me.

She really was between a rock and a hard spot because she could not handle this lifestyle and/or watch me continue to destroy our lives and our marriage. But I continued to not care and just envisioned that our marriage was what it was and finally coming to an end as I previously projected. She never really understood what I was going through because I would never confide in her, other than the physical pain that she could see because I would never let her in on my world. I would always tell her that she would never understand because she never really loved me in the first place. I would just deflect and defer all of my wrongs on her and tell her that she would just be better off without me.

We would continue to separate and get back together because she still loved me but couldn't stand to see me this way or continue to be treated so poorly. My life continued to suffer in every aspect of every meaning of that word. I began getting into problems with coworkers when I did show up to work and that became another issue since we worked at the same place. My lack of showing up for work was actually catching up to me, too, but I would go to my Dr. and play the system to get the appropriate paperwork to miss work and just stay under the radar from losing my job.

Don't get me wrong, I did have a legit medical condition causing depression, anxiety, migraines, bowel issues, etc. I was becoming a successful person at playing Russian roulette with my life, our marriage, other relationships, and everything else in my life. I was on this crash course that I just couldn't find my way out of this time. I just kept feeling sorry for myself and my situation. I did not understand how to change it and didn't have the desire anymore to try to change it.

One day I was having another one of my horrible episodes with pain, sobbing, and feeling dismal so I didn't go to work. It lasted all day and that night I again asked God to please just take me out of my misery. I told him, "My wife, kids, parents, and all the other important people in my life know that I love them and that I would always be there for them in spirit."

I remember laying there on our bed next to my wife and looking at the reflection of the flickering light on the wall from our fireplace. It was about midnight on a colder than usual night in October and I began sobbing and started praying, "Father GOD, I'm so sorry for my sins, transgressions, and iniquities. I have ruined my life and the lives of my wife, children, parents, and everyone else that has ever loved me. I can't take this anymore. Please take me out of my misery and allow me to go wherever you want me to be, just please make all of this stop now." I ended up finally falling asleep and then awoke the next morning. Again, feeling absolutely horrible and also disappointed with God that He was going to allow me to suffer through another day of agony, distress, and misery.

Shawn gave me a kiss on the forehead as she always did when she left for work on days I didn't get out of bed, said she loved me and went off to work earlier than she use to now that she was working at a new job in Sandusky, Ohio. I didn't know it then, but this was not going to be a usual day. I went back to sleep with the help of heavy doses of my medications. Sometime later that afternoon, Shawn texted me from work as she usually did after allowing me to sleep when I stayed home feeling sick. I texted her back and told her that I surprisingly felt a lot better, like a weight had been lifted off my shoulders.

Shawn came home a few hours later and we sat on the couch in our living room and she started talking to me about our life. She could tell something was different from my text and could see it when she was sitting there talking with me. I told her how I had been struggling with every situation in my life and that I didn't know where to turn or what to do. I finally let her in a little and told her for the first time, with tears running down my face, how I prayed last night for God to please just take me out of my misery and allow whatever His will was to happen to me. I told her I just wanted to die and not suffer any more or have her and the children suffer from the lifestyle that I created and destroyed.

Shawn, also crying, told me how she was fervently praying over me and us every day and especially that particular day during her 45-minute drive to work. She prayed, declaring and decreeing for God to heal me and not allow me, our family, and our marriage to suffer any further from all the illness and terrible situations that were going on in our lives. And she prayed for God to please make me the man, the husband, and father that He intended for me to be — the Godly man that she had been praying for each day and weekly in church. She prayed for our family to be reconciled with Love, Mercy, and Grace. God gave me a new outlook on life that day. Some things would definitely get better, but not totally change for all intended purposes.

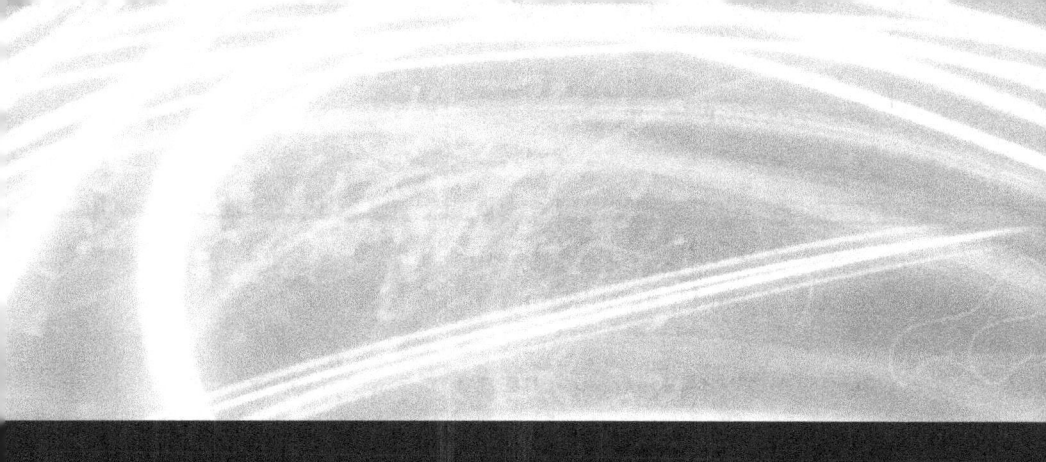

GRAVITATING TO OTHERS

As things started to move in a different flow for our lives, we again began to attend CNC regularly once a week, participating in church programs/small groups and we began to work on our relationship and try to heal our marriage.

We went to counseling with our Pastor, and Shawn also went to different counselors as well to attempt to deal with issues of self-worth that I caused in her life and other issues that I had caused in our marriage. I would also seek counsel through different men's groups within our church, reading scripture, and trying to figure out what had happened to me causing me to get so far off course in my relationship with God.

After a year of beginning to get back on track with our marriage, we were asked to start a small group for couples to just get together and love on one another by our very own Pastor Tina. So, we and two other couples, one older and one younger facilitated this group.

We were reluctant at first knowing all of the things that we had been through in our marriage, but who were we to tell the Pastors wife, "No?" Besides, I felt like I owed something to God for finally taking away my misery and long-suffering.

We would continue this trend for the next several months to almost a year. Then it was like a switch turned and everything went off. I reverted back to the "I'm going to take charge and make everything good again" and the "me" mentality as I saw how other couples within our group were acting toward one another and what was still missing from our relationship. We even went to other couples' groups outside of our church, attending several weekend marriage conferences and came to the realization that our marriage was not like those of other people within these groups or at these marriage conferences.

I longed to have what I previously wanted for all of those years before. To be truly loved, loved for who I am and not what I do. But what I had failed to understand was that the consistent and never-ending barrage of my past actions toward Shawn made her totally reluctant to really and truly allow her guard down around me. I had severely wounded her (like PTSD) and was expecting her to just turn the other cheek once again as she had in the past when I treated her so poorly for years.

Like the Bible says in Matthew 5:39, "But I say to you, do not resist the one who is evil. But if anyone slaps you on the right cheek, turn to him the other also (ESV)." And of course, I was a better husband now and we were working toward making our marriage a better place, so why wouldn't she just forgive me and turn the other cheek?

I continued to ask for forgiveness for all of the years that I was a terrible person and continued to try to make everything right with her. It just wasn't moving at the pace that I had hoped it would. I would recognize my actions when I started to act out of character and seek clemency from God as well.

But again, I continued to teeter in and out of these thoughts that there is no way that she will ever be able to forgive me for all of the things that I have said, names that I have called her, things that I've done to her, or how I acted toward her. I treated her so poorly for so many years, there was probably no hope for us to truly survive our past. At least my past actions. No matter how hard I tried to make the past go away, tell her how much I loved her, thanked her for not giving up on us, or that I was truly sorry for what I put her through, it never seemed to make a difference. She had put up this wall around her heart and I could do nothing about it.

I felt like she had died somewhere along the journey, too, and she didn't even realize it. I believed that our marriage was on the ropes again and I was just a spectator watching helplessly as she had to battle all of these demons I created. She continued to struggle with the past for the next year and she was just existent in our marriage, never happy, and never out from under the consistent pressure again. But this time it was to finally forgive me.

My only hope was that one day she would be able to see the real me and that things were going to be better. I had gotten a new job and things were getting back together for us financially once again. We continued to trek along through the everyday ups and downs of life and marriage, but we still were never on the same page. We would have several good days in a row and then I would slip and revert and take a step backward. But to Shawn, it was like going all the way back to the beginning each and every time something like this would happen. It would instantaneously remind her of the tragic past.

She was so frail and shell-shocked that I believe she was truly suffering from a form of PTSD. Every time something sounded too familiar or if I even joked about something I did in the past, her mind would race back and she would become a different person almost instantaneously. I couldn't even say anything to the effect of, "Well, that's stupid" or "Why would you think that?" Those words would be translated in her mind to "You're dumb or ignorant" and "That's not how you should be thinking, what's wrong with you?" And these are just a few of the simple examples of her mind racing to a negative thought process about herself because she was never allowed to be herself.

She was never allowed to make a simple mistake without hearing a negative response from me. She was required to be who I wanted her to be, never messing up or making a mistake and not who she really was, her true self. This again went on for about another year of me pressing her for forgiveness, banging my own drum of how I acted in a certain situation, or how I treated her in another circumstance and would follow up with saying, "Aren't you glad that I don't treat you like that anymore?"

Another negative effect on our marriage is how I treated her in the bedroom. I thought that as soon as I won her good graces after the first few months, everything would be good when it came to our intimate relationship in the bedroom. Talk about leaving a lasting effect on a person's mind! I guess I never understood the negative impact that I was making on her all of those years.

A wife is supposed to feel safe and secure in the arms of her husband, but I had created a shell-shocked young woman that would shudder whenever intimacy was a thought process let alone a reality. She was always looking over her shoulder for the hammer to fall in that totally embarrassing and uncomfortable situation, or the thought and imagery of someone watching.

But the better our relationship became and the closer we as a couple became while attempting to overcome our past, the more intimate I expected our relationship to grow. And yet, Shawn needed to move at a much slower pace creating very awkward and sometimes painful memories.

Unfortunately, when I would push to become more intimate, the more she would resist because she was having difficulty with past pornography and videoing. I guess I felt like we had moved beyond this in our reconciled relationship, but I was the only one on that page and began to have more setbacks in my behavior, becoming more impatient with her to get over the past.

Thus, I began to think with more and more negativity about our marriage and that we were never going to get past this. And of course, there is always pressure from the Prince of Darkness and the ideologies that there may be a better situation or person elsewhere. He proposes that we think we are not right with Gods' plan, and living out our Christian walk with Him. I spoke of the new job, which was a good thing financially, but that meant other women who would be potential suitors of an outside relationship.

I was really beginning to struggle again with my past and demons haunting me along with the mistakes that I created in our marriage. I was hoping that they would have vanished by now and we would already be to the "happily ever after" part of our life as well. But we weren't getting any closer and I was ready to chalk it up as a lost cause and move on.

I think I was truly okay with this because I remember thinking several times throughout our dysfunctional marriage that when we first got married, I was just in it to be married to this hot little thing and the true commitment to God was really never there from the beginning. Yes, we said our vows before a Minister but did either of us ever really mean them or take them seriously?

I was never sure, and at this point in our marriage, I still really never knew. I only knew that the first 12-plus years were more of just an ongoing relationship with lots of ups and downs, fighting, sex, and of course many fun times partying with friends. The next three-plus years seemed to be a battlefield of landmines of past dilemma's and trying to break the bondage of our past mistakes. Were either of us in this for the right reason anyway? Were we really supposed to be husband and wife? Or was it time to see it for what it was and how it looked from the beginning.

They always say that opposition and darkness come before a breakthrough. Just like darkness before dawn, and that darkness has to give way to light! Also, keep in mind, the greater the Breakthrough, the stronger the opposition will come at you and your circumstances.

The devil didn't want us to embark on the journey that we were about to take and he was going to do everything in his power to once again ruin several aspects of our lives. He sought to manipulate our thinking to deem me/us unworthy because of our past mistakes, trials, and iniquities.

ESCAPING COMMITMENT WITH BIBLICAL REASONING

Both of us continued to make mistakes with being embattled in a fight that was already won. But neither of us could escape the chains, shackles, or curses that I or we had put on our marriage or each other.

So we attempted to continue forging onward in our marriage and not let anyone know that things were still amiss in our lives or our marriage. We continued to be a part of the now called Couples Connecting small group, the one that I fore-mentioned through our church. During this time all of these situations and preconceived notions we were battling in both of our minds were ongoing. But neither of us would tell anyone any more than what the Pastor already knew in our previous counseling sessions.

We continued to battle our demons separately and moved on with our dysfunctional married life like this is what God wanted for us. We were then asked by other couples to start doing study groups in our monthly get together, but then that would require us to meet more frequently. We and the older couple, Marty and Eydie, decided we would do a "Fireproof" study group first.

This should be an easy starter since Shawn and I were already familiar with these sessions since this was one of the previous couple's weekend retreats we had attended. And we personally knew the couple that facilitated that conference so we could always get pointers from Roz and Heather too. So we began with approximately 15 other couples signing up to participate.

This went very well and it seemed as if we were getting back on the right track again. As we dove more deeply into this Fireproof study guide and clips, the more and more I found the similarity of those same characters to our actual life. All of the situations that were ethical dilemmas to these characters in this movie were all of my ethical dilemmas of our past. My life was a real-life dramatization of this movie and the ensuing problems related to these unethical decisions.

But the good thing was that in the movie, they made it above and beyond these situations and circumstances to be even closer to God and one another, totally reconciling their marriage into happily ever after. This was exactly what I had always wanted for my life! Things continued to go well and we continued to discuss each week how we were able to overcome these situations and circumstances just like what was able to be achieved in the study material. It was a textbook process and ending.

Boom, drop the mic! We finally made it right ... happily ever after, THE END. Just like the movie! Well, hold your horses. We were okay as a couple and continuing to try day after day to be our better selves and move forward.

We continued to meet monthly in our group and again it was brought up that we did such a great job with the first study group and were so amazingly transparent, that these same couples wanted us to do another one, and then another one after that. The second was "Love Languages" and the third was "Apologies." What an eye-opening experience that we were not prepared for at all! I thought that because we were so good at the first study group, it was just a matter of reading the material and then answering the questions proposed with everyone each week. All we would do is assist in the facilitation of the questions and let it go from there. This went fairly well at first.

But what we were totally unprepared for is that all of these questions would raise other questions in our own marriage, like why we were truly together and what really made our marriage fulfilling to us. WOW, what an amazing study group for couples to truly be a part of. But it will raise some very interesting questions. And you better be ready and willing to accept your spouse's answers with a grain of salt.

The further we moved into the second study, the more I was feeling unfulfilled and my "Love Tank" was empty, probably because it had a hole in it. I thought without a doubt that I was overfilling Shawn's all of the time, but found out otherwise through her perspectives and past resentments. I did not fill her love tank, because it was either very watered down, unsafe territory, or even volatile to her to even properly receive.

I knew exactly what her interests and needs were, but I was also an expert at manipulating them and she knew that. So with what good reason would she want to pour into my life and our relationship if it was superficial to her. It all looked good on the outside, warm and fuzzy, but what if it was rotten on the inside? And we were still fresh in our new commitment to each other and trying to work things out.

The third study group on the Apologies was just plain ugly behind the scenes for us. We never had a disagreement in front of anyone at the studies, nor did anyone ever know that we were seriously struggling with this study, but there was one time in the parking lot about thirty minutes before a session was to begin that we almost just left because of an argument. And it was about halfway through this book study that I'm sure my tone at times was like, "Right Shawn!" ... calling her out in front of everyone.

And Shawn would just cringe and tighten up like a clam. I was still hounding her for "Forgiveness" and especially throughout this entire study session, I felt like she just needed to get over whatever was still going on in her mind. If she truly loved me and truly forgave me like she said she did while we were in counseling, then that should be sufficient for us to move forward in our relationship. So I continued to batter her with fact after fact each week during the rest of the "Apologies" sessions on why I deserved forgiveness, redemption, and freedom from this stranglehold that she continued to have on me and our marriage.

It was time to break the chains of the past, forgive me, and move forward in God's plans for "Us" as a couple. Or at least my plans as I continued to hammer her with book after book from famous Evangelical authors about prayer for others, forgiving through the movie aforementioned, mind battles, things that steal from you, stopping pain, stealing joy, etc.

But the more I pushed again for her to understand, the more Shawn became reluctant to pursue any interest in reading these books, let alone hear my take of what these authors were suggesting to her. Besides the fact that it was coming from a motive which was single-minded and not entirely the way it was meant to be taken. This continued for about another year but I was also beginning to struggle with another battle that I was not prepared to endure and was becoming ever more prevalent in my life.

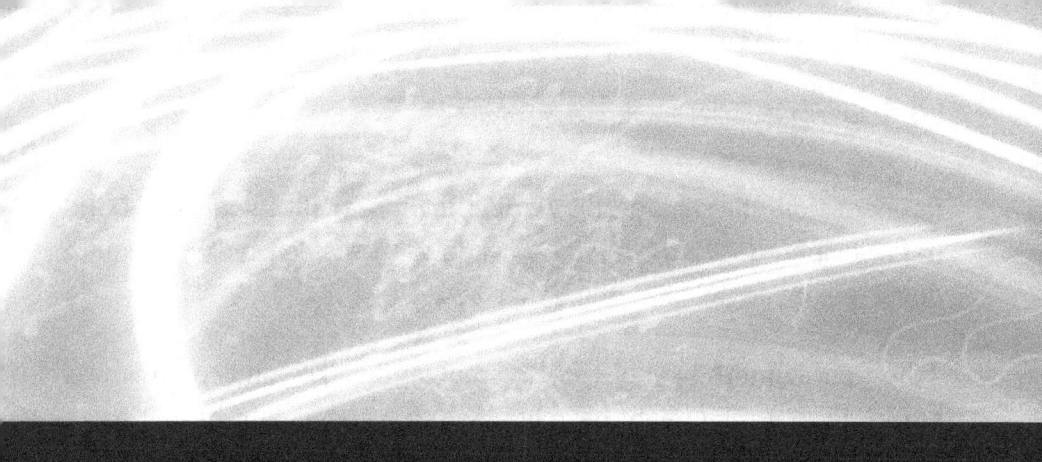

DYING SLOWLY WITHIN

I had come to another crossroad in my life, and in my marriage. Again, I was feeling totally helpless and didn't understand. Why do I continue to struggle with this inner battle where I continue to teeter back and forth between what I know and what I feel is right to me? What God has intended for me to be and where he was taking our marriage, and then it all just falls flat like it was never supposed to be in the first place.

The struggle is so hard sometimes, and I know it's real because I've personally dealt with it several times in my life. It would continue to rear its ugliness and feed my inner being with feelings of freedom, worth, desire, lust, self-satisfaction, greed, thoughts of grandeur, delusions, etc.

The further I would go in my walk to become closer with God, the more prevalent these items from my past would rear their ugliness.

The more I learned of the desires of what God has for me and the true freedom from the ways of this world, the more that the Prince of Darkness whispered, "It's ok, no one will know, no one can see what you're doing, go ahead it's ok to think that way."

"The thief cometh not, but for to steal, and to kill, and to destroy; I am come that they might have life, and that they might have it more abundantly" (John 10:10 KJV).

Whenever I thought that I had handled these issues and put them in my past and locked them away for good, they would come back at me even harder and with more vengeance. Every time I thought that I had control of my inner thoughts, the thief showed me my past miscues, playing reel to reel tapes of everything that I had ever done wrong.

The Prince of Darkness said, "You think God will forgive you for this?" He reminded me of pornographic images I have seen in the past. He clouded my thinking and made me feel embarrassed and unworthy of my actions behind my wife's back. He would incite me to re-live conversations that I had with some of those promiscuous women of the past and try to get me to believe that this kind of life can be better somewhere else or with someone else.

And then someone at work says something to remind you of your past thoughts. When an image appears in your email, you immediately revert back to a do or die situation. Do I, or don't I? I was continually at battle with my mind, soul, and past life mistakes.

I continued to think about what I have done, said, or hid so no one would think ill-mannered of me. I tried to make everything seem to be on the up and up and basically living a lie each and every day. Then I would believe that he was right in one moment and wrong in the next. These thoughts slowly made my hope die that our marriage would survive all of this again.

The battles and arguments needed to stop and stop for good, or it would be the end of us once and for all. I couldn't imagine quitting after we had invested so much time and energy into restoring our marriage, going to counseling sessions, being a part of these small groups. But it was again a never-ending cycle that just didn't seem to be broken or dismantled as I thought. I did love her but was this really all worth everything that we were going through? I continued to go to Bible studies on Spiritual Warfare, complete book studies on Manhood, and how to become a better role model with our campus pastor, Pastor Jim.

Here are some of the notes that I took during those study group sessions at CNC. Satan always fights in darkness, and there are several signs that it's a Spiritual battle vs. just a mere mistake. He has a specific area he's attacking, so you need to become aware of the starting point to know precisely what you are battling.

1. He will attempt to severe through a planned attack or major change in your life situation.
2. Your temptation to sin will be far beyond your normal actions. (Acts of Grandeur)
3. He will allow for a pattern of reoccurring negative events to commence in or around your life.

4. He will not allow Love, Peace, Joy, or Righteousness to prevail.
5. You will have severe discouragements. You will know that something is amiss and not feel right in your life.
6. Condemnation to the point that it cripples your critical thinking and clouds your thoughts of forgiveness.
7. He will intimidate you with fear and attempt to persuade you that God's plans are not right for you.
8. He thrives on confusion where communication is distorted or misrepresented.
9. He applies pressure on your most important relationships.
10. It's a never-ending battle in your mind. It just plays over and over with negativity.

I was definitely in a spiritual battle, and I was not prepared to defend my own life, let alone my marriage or any member of my family! He was after me and my marriage. When he wasn't able to succeed, he came even harder in yet another area in my life. This caused me to become entrenched in the most challenging physical fight I would endure to this point in my life. Don't think for a moment that just because he can't destroy or kill this one area in your life that he won't come back. *"Like a lion that is greedy of his prey, and as it were a young lion lurking in secret places"* (Psalm 17:12 ESB).

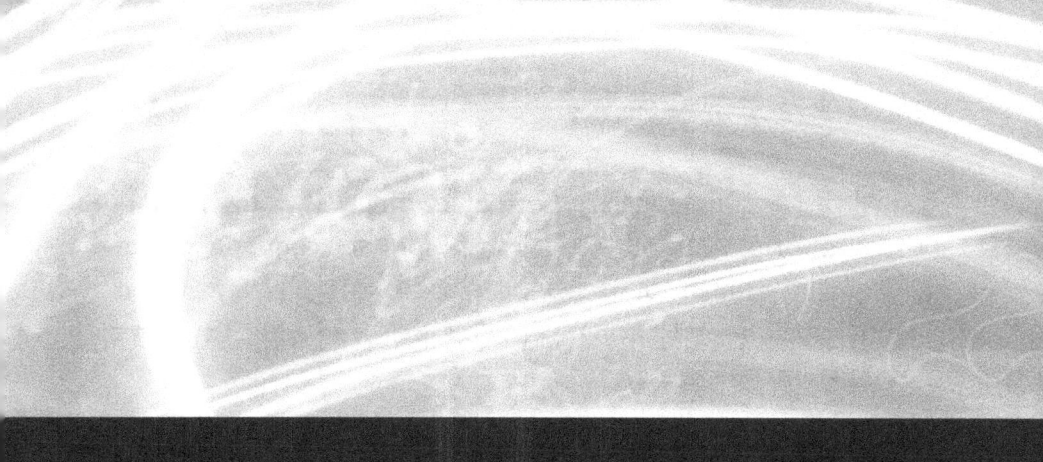

MEDICAL ISSUES AND DEATH

I had begun to struggle with some back issues from my past since the very first study group. With everyone well aware of my inability to move efficiently as I had before, the couples decided at the study group to gather around me to lay hands and pray over me after one of our first couples sessions.

I had previously been in a terrible auto accident back in 2003. I was hit from behind on a highway by a semi-truck. The accident forced me off the right side of the road and across a six feet wide by three foot deep ditch. I slid across snowy grass approximately 150' and in between two pine trees. I finally stopped after I literally bounced off of the house at this property. I was injured in my lower back and eventually had surgery to correct the issues via bilateral discectomy and bilateral laminectomy, making my back incredibly unstable for the future.

Thirteen years after the fact, my back was starting to collapse and impinging my L5-S1 vertebral nerves causing tremendous pain in my back and down my left leg. One day at work, I was attempting to walk down the hallway, and someone said, "What's wrong with you?" I said nothing, not really knowing but had my suspicions and continued down the hallway. By the time I got to the end of about a 40' hallway, I was dragging my left foot and having incredible pain and couldn't even take another step.

I immediately was taken from work to the ER, and the diagnoses were an impinged nerve and drop foot. After two weeks of Chiropractic treatment and therapy, I was not getting any better. I was then referred to and started to follow up with a neurosurgeon, and surgery was the final recommendation. After a long drawn out process and battle with an insurance company, my insurance company finally approved the surgery.

I ended up having a surgical process on my lumbar spine at L5-S1 implanting a cage to complete a spinal fusion on my two vertebrae. Basically, what happens is they took four screws with holes in the one end for a rod to slide through and screwed two of them into each side of my L5 and S1 vertebra. Each of these screws have a steel rod fed from top to bottom on each side of my spine and tightened to not allow instability and slippage. This was a grueling five, almost six hour process, and $100,000 procedure. Thank God that the insurance company approved the surgery … or so I thought.

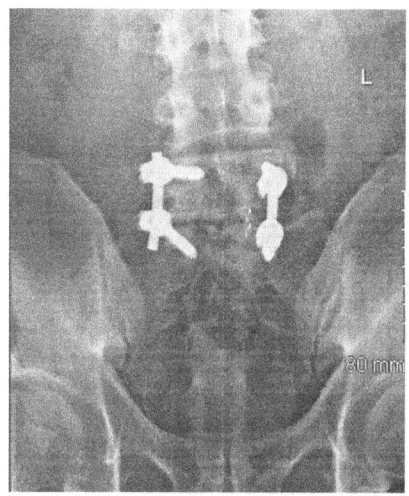

Recovery from surgery was a two-day hospital stay from the surgery. Still, the ensuing therapy would be a long, grueling, and tedious process. The plan was that I would go for treatment three times a week to begin and was making reasonably good progress to start, but then all progress stopped. The pain started to worsen and my limp returned. So did the drop foot, forcing me to walk with a cane to maintain my balance. A spinal back brace for increased core stability.

Procedure after procedure was being completed while therapy also continued: EMG, X-rays, spinal blocks, steroid injections, pain patches, pain management appointments, increased pain medications, and nerve blockers to no avail.

A whirlwind of pain, numbness, medication, and suffering ensued daily. I was completely and utterly miserable every second of every day unless I was in my recliner chair in our living room with ice on my lumbar area and having the chair in a reclined position. My feet had to be elevated to relieve the pressure on my spine.

I was on so many medications, and the combination of some of these medications were making me hallucinate. I had increased and very volatile bouts of anger and rage, even worse than anyone had ever seen in me before. No one except Shawn would even want to be around me, and then sometimes not even her. She would go to another area of the so-called "mansion" just to get away from me. I was completely debilitated, miserable, and heartbroken.

Our finances again diminished to nothing as I could not work. Still, I eventually received long-term disability pay (60%) from my job to barely keep us afloat with all of our household expenses and new medical bills.

We had to seek outside help from family members financially. Then again came along our wonderful CNC church family to help us get landscaping assistance and other things such as meals. Shawn now had to try to manage work, household duties, finances, and of course, taking care of me.

I even wondered if this is why I worked in therapy for all of those years, to effectively know how to help take care of myself and how to use all of the adaptive equipment that I needed to assist with getting dressed each day. Shawn had to rearrange her entire life, including her work schedule to help me get dressed before leaving for work each day as I got worse. She had to get me to and from physician and therapy appointments. What a load on your spouse to try to endure! Talk about unconditional love!

And try taking care of a person who's treated you so poorly and taken advantage of you throughout your entire marriage too. Meanwhile, I tried to stay upbeat about my circumstance. I again turned to the Bible for guidance and, for the first time, had read the entire Bible from cover to cover.

While reading, I kept thinking that I continuously felt like Jonah and my house was the whale. But I could never grasp the concept of what I was reading or thinking. I continued to read, battle, cry, become frustrated with everyone, cry, become angry at God, and cry some more. I kept asking Shawn, "Why is this happening to me?" She would continue to pray for me and with me. I would pray and read and read and pray.

I slowly kept getting worse each day and slowly dying more on the inside until finally, one day, I snapped. I just couldn't take it anymore, and the slightest little thing had set me off more than usual. It was July 19, 2017, and it was raining hard that day, and one of our outside sump pumps kept getting stuck for some reason. Shawn kept trying to do her best at managing all of the household circumstances, and it was all finally getting to her as well. She was very frustrated and upset that she wasn't able to make ends meet. I started getting mad that she couldn't do a simple household task that I had done so many times before in a few seconds.

We were both standing out in the downpouring rain as I was trying to give her pointers with an attitude on how to make the pump work again. She still couldn't get it to work, so I got mad as always and told her to get the "F" out of the way and get her fat ass back inside since she couldn't fix it. I'll just find someone to do it even if I have to break my back and do it myself. Wounded and heartbroken, she just hung her head, walked away, and began to take her boots off and go back inside as I demanded.

As I was attempting to come back inside, I noticed that she left her muck boots outside and they were literally collecting rainwater. As I went into the house, I yelled at her again with even more anger, frustration, and attitude. "What the hell are you thinking of leaving your boots out in the rain? Are you collecting water to see how much rain we're getting?" Not knowing what to say, she just turned and walked away with no response to finish the laundry that she had previously started in another room.

As I was making my way back to my recliner in extreme pain, angered and pissed off at her, and soaked, I continued to make ill-mannered comments about her not being able to do something that was supposedly so simple.

And those comments became the final straw. Shawn had had all she could possibly take of me, myself, and I! Not that those were ridiculous or wrong questions to ask, but it was the wrong moment. It was with anger, the sound of stupidity, and failure that I had expressed so many times before throughout our marriage and in all of our other previous arguments. All of this pressure, stress, circumstances, and anger from the past came flooding back instantaneously.

She threw the laundry basket down, grabbed the car keys, and said, "I'M DONE. I can't do this anymore," then turned and walked out the door. Angry at her and the situation, I said, "Good riddance, I don't need you, and don't let the door hit your ass on the way out of my life!"

At that point, I thought that she was just mad as always and would be back sometime throughout the night or the next day, just like all of the other times that we had fought. I didn't hear from her at all the following morning. She called later that afternoon and said that she was coming by to pick up a few things and that she would stay somewhere for a while until she could figure some things out.

So, she came and picked up some of her clothes and personal care items and then left again. I was not sure what to think other than this was for sure, the final nail in our marriage coffin. So I tried my best to take care of myself and continue to convince myself that all I needed was me, myself, and I and that I would be fine.

I would just get in touch with my parents, children, or a friend and see if they could help me if I needed anything until Shawn decided what she wanted to do next. I continued to read inspirational books to try to keep my mind preoccupied and just try to take care of myself the best that I could, but I was failing miserably. And I still continued having that same thought about Jonah and the whale, and yet not understanding.

A few weeks went by, and I rarely if ever heard from or saw Shawn. I knew that things were probably done for us and our marriage. She was done, I was done, and I thought that God was perhaps done too. Our marriage was on life support at its best, and the only thing left to do was for one of us to pull the proverbial plug. I tried to go on with life even though it had no meaning. I missed my best friend too.

One day as I was staring out the big picture window that my recliner sat beside, since my children wanted me to be able to see the world and not be so isolated in our bedroom. As I sat and looked at the world and my life, I saw how I had created this wonderful place to isolate myself and everyone. I was always pushing them all away, including God. I just started sobbing and apologized to God for being a terrible person. I asked Him what I could have done to be a better husband, father, son, and friend to all of them.

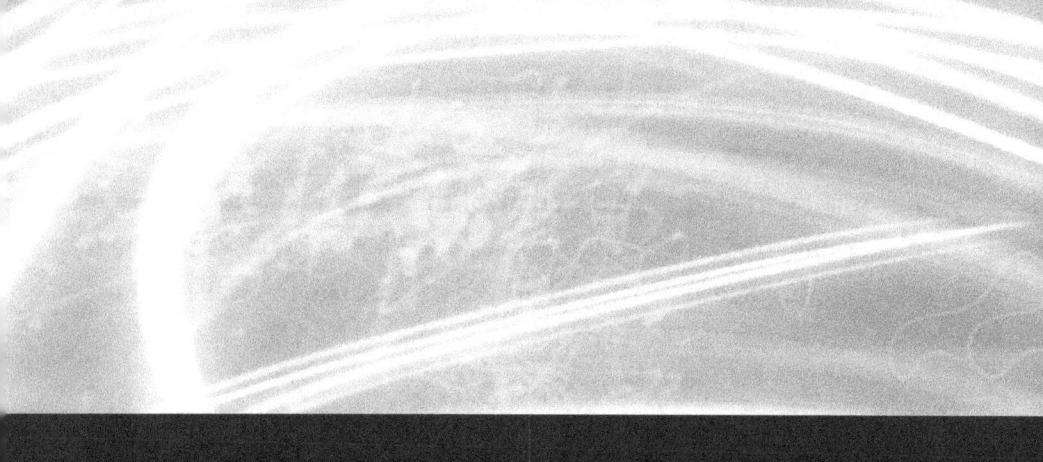

YOUR ETERNAL LIGHT

Sunday, July 30, 2017, I woke up from the reclining chair as I did every day and decided to try to get ready to attend the 10 AM service at CNC. It took me quite a while to get prepared as I was all by myself. This would be the first time I would try to attend church services by myself since this entire incident with my back had happened.

We usually just watched services via podcasts on our phones and rarely attended services together as it was just way too much for me to endure. This particular day I felt a stronger than normal desire that I needed to get closer to God, and the only way that I knew how to do that was to go to the altar. I managed to drive myself to CNC on Leavitt Rd. in Lorain, Ohio, which was a feat in itself considering that I could barely walk by myself with a cane, a back brace, and a terrible limp secondary to my drop foot.

I tried to get there as early as I could to be there through praise and worship before hearing the word. While listening to the inspirational and beautiful songs, I struggled to stand up with my back brace and cane. Still, I was able to give God all of the praise that I had left in my broken mind, body, and soul. As I was standing to praise God, I heard an ever small voice say to me, "Tell Rafael that I love the way he praises me and to keep it up" "and come."

Rafael is a younger man, maybe in his late 20s or early 30s that is challenged and always attended CNC, to my knowledge. I didn't know him and really didn't care to get to know him at this point in my life.

He usually sat on the same side of the church that we sat, and I only knew him by the first name and would occasionally say "Hello" or "Hi," if we made eye contact. This day, Rafael praised God even more abundantly and outspokenly as he always did and was next to me when I stood.

I didn't know it then, but this was the last time I saw Rafael for almost a year. So, as requested, I said, "Excuse me" to Rafael as I attempted to step around him to go to the altar. Since he always stands up close to the chair in front of him, I stepped behind him, placed my hand on his shoulder, and then leaned to his ear and said, "Rafael, keep up the good work. God loves the way you praise Him." He replied, "Thanks man!" as he does quite often, and then I hobbled to the altar with my cane.

As I got to the altar, all I can remember is hearing overwhelming beautiful music. I started to sob profusely while raising my right hand and hanging on to the cane with my left hand and feeling so entirely broken and lost. I began to pray, "Father God, please forgive me of my sins, transgressions, and iniquities. Please do Your perfect will and Your perfect way in every area of my life and allow me to be the Son that You have created me to be."

I continued to stand and love Him with ALL my heart and praised Him through my tears and brokenness with my head bowed. I then returned to my seat at the end of the songs, still struggling to get back to my seat. I attempted to sit on the cushioned chair that felt like I was sitting on a wooden plank next to Rafael in the congregation.

I sat there and listened to Dr. Louis Kayatin preach a message on Acts Chapter 3, you know, the one with the lame man that was outside the Temple begging for alms. The lame were not allowed to enter the gates or the church because they were deemed unfit and unworthy. I immediately thanked God at that very moment, saying, "Thank you, God, for not having or allowing these rules today. You have deemed me worthy and able to be in Your presence and in this church to honor You."

Acts 3:6-8 NIV: "Then Peter said, Silver and gold have I none: but such as I have give I thee: In the name of Jesus Christ of Nazareth rise up and walk. And he took him by the right hand, and lifted him up: and immediately his feet and ankle bones received strength. And he leaping up, stood, and entered with them into the temple, walking, and leaping, and praising God."

I listened to the remainder of the service. I then made my way out of the seats to leave ever so slowly and remember it, taking every ounce of my strength to get back to the truck. As I reached the aisle, I was approached by one of the ushers that I didn't really know very well but had seen many times before. He asked how I was doing and if there was anything that he could do to help me out. I said that I'm doing ok and that I'll make it. I told him what the doctors had said to me at my last appointment, and his response was, "Do you know what the middle of the Bible says?" I responded that I did not know. He said it's Psalms 118:8 "It is better to take refuge in the LORD than to trust in humans." And with that, I said goodbye and headed to my truck.

I eventually got home and into the house, which was another feat itself, considering I had to negotiate 3 steps with no railing, opening a door at the top, all while maintaining my balance with a single point cane. Although I managed and was thoroughly exhausted, to say the least, considering that this was the most movement that I had completed in quite some time. But I was determined. I sat and rested for about an hour in the recliner and then decided that I would get something to drink because my medications always made me extremely thirsty.

So I got up, got a glass out of the kitchen cabinet, and started filling it up with water from the refrigerator door water dispenser. As I began to fill the glass with water, I looked toward our front door at about the 1 o'clock position on a clock from where I was standing. As I began to look at the front entrance, a white light began to show ever so vibrantly. It started radiantly flooding light rapidly everywhere throughout the entire room so that everything was completely white with no exact dimensions as if I were standing inside of a cloud.

I couldn't see anything but this pure, intense white light. Then I had this magnificent feeling of warmth and flowing sensation over my entire body. It felt so amazing, comfortable, and refreshing. It was the best feeling that I have ever had in my whole life. I had never experienced or encountered such an Amazing presence before, and it seemed like I could just stay there forever and be entirely at Peace.

And in what seemed like forever, I then realized that I was back in my kitchen with the glass of water still up to the dispenser. Water was running over the edge of the glass, on my hand, down the front of the fridge, and all over the floor, creating about a 2-3' puddle of water around my feet. I immediately stopped filling the glass, spilling some more water on the floor, and sat it down on the countertop. I then reached to my left about 5' away to grab a towel hanging on the stove handle. I then bent down and started wiping the water that was all over the floor.

Still enamored with that amazing white light, the warmth and comfort of that feeling, I finished cleaning the water off the floor and then walked into our bedroom. I kicked my shoes off my feet since they were wet from spilling and standing in the water.

I was thinking about that wonderful and fulfilling feeling of comfort and warmth. I then bent down from a standing position, bending my knees to kneel on one knee and bending my back to grab my shoes to put them under the end of the bed where I always kept them. I then knelt on both knees bending even further toward the floor to see where I was reaching to put my shoes in the correct space under the bed. As I was reaching, I then realized what I had just done.

Wait a minute, I just cleaned up that water, I just walked into the bedroom with no cane, and now I was kneeling at the end of my bed and sobbing, saying. "THANK YOU, JESUS, I'M HEALED!" I then jumped to my feet, still sobbing in pure joy, and raised both of my arms with thankfulness and glee, shouting, "THANK YOU, FATHER GOD, FOR HEALING ME!" "I AM HEALED!" "I AM HEALED!"

I then pulled the back brace off and ran back to the kitchen where my cell phone was charging. I immediately called Shawn to tell her of the Miracle and of the Amazing white light that I had experienced. So I frantically told her all that had happened, talking about 100 miles an hour. She said, "Oh, ok, but I'm busy right now celebrating my family members being water baptized. I'll call you later."

I then called my children one by one, my parents, Shawn's parents, Dr. Kayatin, all my friends, everyone that I could think of telling. They all kept telling me the same thing. You what? Slow down, wait a minute. No pain, nothing? That's so amazing and awesome. Praise God! They were all ecstatic for my miracle healing.

While speaking to Dr. Kayatin, he told me in that very moment that he felt that the Holy Spirit was telling him to convey to me that God was not done writing my story. There was more to come. There was still a blessing to come to fruition.

Day turned into night, night turned to day. I still didn't get a return call from Shawn. I didn't get to talk to her until later the next evening when I actually called her, and she seemed so short and doubtful, like what's the catch, what stunt are you trying to pull now. But that's okay because I was Healed and out and about showing all of my family and friends. I was Healed, Whole, and Healthy, just like the beggar outside the temple wall.

I was ecstatic and could not let enough people know what God had done in, with, through, to, and upon me. I even drove all the way to Columbus the next day to see our eldest son to show him in person that I was completely and totally healed. And still, I had minimal to no contact from Shawn. But that was totally ok because I knew that I was fully and completely loved by God for the first time in my entire life, and THAT was enough. Yes, me, Jeffrey Allen Lind. I finally, for the first time in my life, knew exactly who I am to Him. I am His son, and He is, the Great, I AM!

> Maybe the journey isn't so much about becoming anything. Maybe it's about un-becoming everything that isn't really you so you can be who you were meant to be in the first place.

LOVING ME FOR WHO I AM AND KNOWING WHO I AM

To this very day, I continue to be amazed at what God has done to and for me. A few days after He healed me, I sat on my bedroom floor and just talked to Him like He was in the room with me that day. Like there was a connection from my heart to Him. At that very moment, I realized that everything that I was encountering was because I didn't really know who He was, who I was, and who I am to Him.

It was a matter of my heart and not physicality at all, but Spiritually and Emotionally. I had an issue with coming to Him without expectation and need. I was not thankful or grateful. When we are thankful for the things that He has given us and grateful for the things we have, there is great satisfaction and contentment far beyond all understanding.

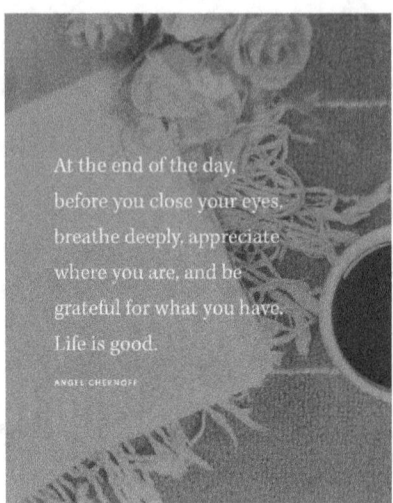

And the constant state of feeling like Jonah and my house being the whale, I was running from God at every turn just like Jonah was trying to run from Him.

We serve a God of Second Chances, *"... and the word of the Lord came unto Jonah the second time" (Jonah 1).* Jonah tried to run from God, but God wouldn't let him.

I was always trying to run from God just like Jonah and trying to be something that I was never meant to be, and trying to create the next best thing or situation in my life. I knew of God and who He was, but I would try to pick and choose God when I wanted Him and then try to put my own spin on how I wanted things to work out.

This is obviously not how God wanted things to be in my life. My heart was always in the wrong place. *Jeremiah 17:9-10 KJV: "The heart is deceitful above all things, and desperately wicked: who can know it? I the Lord search the heart, I try the reins, even to give every man according to his ways, and according to the fruit of his doings."* My heart was in the wrong place most of my life, even though God had shown His grace and mercy several times throughout my life.

I call my condition Myopia (this causes distant objects to be blurry while close objects appear normal, Wikipedia) of the heart. I chose to be near-sighted in my heart, allowing the world to be ever so close and God to be distantly blurry unless I needed Him. Well, that also translated to the way that I thought, felt, and responded to everything.

I would only see things from a limited perspective. If you, the idea, the thought, the circumstance, etc ... didn't fit within that 45-degree perspective (that I have since dubbed as Jeffision), then I didn't like it, or want anything to do with it. I would even tell people that I didn't like bacon, peanut butter, ice cream, anything grape- or ranch-flavored because it wasn't something that I particularly liked or wanted.

As I continued making poor choice after poor choice, He still chose to love me no matter what. He never gave up on me. *Matthew 18:12: "If a man has a hundred sheep, and one of them be gone astray, does he not leave the ninety and nine, and go into the mountains, and seek that which is gone astray?"*

And this is precisely what He has done for me. No matter what I did, no matter how many times I seemed to mess up, no matter how big of

a mess I made of all situations in my life, He never gave up on me. He never stopped searching for me. He was always there. I just needed to surrender all and allow Him to do His perfect will and His perfect way in, with, to, through, and upon my life each and every day.

In those very moments, I knew exactly who I was and am. His child. I said it that same day He healed me, and I still know and say it every day.

"I AM A CHILD OF GOD!" But it didn't and wasn't going to happen until I surrendered ALL to Him. Surrendering all that I am, all of the people I love, all that I have, and ALL Control.

It took me humbly and solemnly going to Him at the altar, right to the foot of the cross, waving that proverbial white flag. I said, "I surrender. I can't do this anymore. I quit trying to control my life and trying to manipulate and control everyone and everything that I am a part of."

This is where the title of this book comes from — I was "Out of Control." Because He is now in control of my life.

And this is another message from God to put these very words into print to tell everyone of my healing by His Grace and Love. He has given me another chance at life to spread His Good news.

The end of John 10:10 NKJV states, *"I have come that they may have life, and that they may have it more abundantly."* Once I surrendered ALL to Him, my heart was wide open like flood gates to receive His amazing, unconditional Love. And from there, my mind followed suit, and of course, my body followed right behind.

Proverbs 23:7 KJV: "For as he thinks in his heart, so is he." I know that God had a plan for me all along, but I had to let go of my plan to control and not try to manipulate His plan for it to come to fruition. *Jeremiah 29:11 NKJ: "For I know the thoughts that I think toward you, said the LORD, thoughts of peace, and not of evil, to give you the end you wait for."*

Proverbs 3:5-6 NKJ: "Trust in the LORD with all thy heart; and lean not unto your own understanding." And now, I allow God to be in total control over my life and lead me through life just like my favorite verse, Psalms 23. This was always my favorite chapter of the Bible, and I never knew why. Still, it was always the most reassuring and comforting to me and perfectly depicts how we, as Christians, need to leave God in control and lead us through our daily walk.

INVESTING IN FAITH, PRAYER, AND DONNING MY ARMOR

As I continued to have faith and believe in God's plan for my life to be healed entirely, and now in my new walk with Him, I began with prayer. I pray for and over others, in the morning, throughout the day, and at night.

I also began telling my Physicians, Nurse practitioners, and other medical staff that were treating me throughout this trying time in my life all about what God has done for me, His love, and how he healed me. With a lot of skepticism and bewildered looks from most medical staff and therapists, I had one particular CNP, while in tears, tell me how I was such an inspiration to her, her faith, and how my healing was so heartfelt. She said she would never forget my story of God's amazing love. I told her that it wasn't me, but God in me who touched her heart.

I just continue to tell everyone, distant family, friends, and everyone I would or still encounter. I even had a few people approach me about my healing and wanting me to give my testimony at their respective churches. Still, I knew that there was a more significant meaning and greater testimony to come. This would be the testimony of how God not only healed, saved, and changed me, but healed another heart and ultimately saved the Covenant of Our marriage.

I mentioned before how Shawn was remaining distant and uncertain of my healing. She actually was in downright disbelief at first. There were many family including her parents, friends, and others that had seen me and would tell her how good I looked, spoke about God and my healing, responded to adversity, accepted full responsibility for our separation, established new relationships within CNC, and at work, etc… Still, she would tell them, "You can buy into it but not me." Do you remember the old adage, "Fool me once, shame on you, fool me twice, shame on me."

Well, there wasn't going to be another chance to fool her since she never knew when I was honest or when I was full of it and trying to smooth things over. I mean, I could've been a great used car salesman in my previous lifetime. No, she was finally away from it all and didn't want to think about or have to deal with any part of our messy marriage. She was going to concentrate on her and only her. I get it. She finally could be herself, feel free, not having to watch what she did. She didn't have to be concerned with being condemned for her actions or hearing any condescending comments spew from my mouth.

She was doing things her way, but still leaning on God for answers/solution and weathering the storms of our past and currently in her life.

Likewise, I, too, was divulging deep into the Word to know Him more and to understand the reasons why our marriage was on its last chance. Not that I didn't have a clue since I was now able to see from a much clearer perspective rather than when I had mentioned the "Myopia of my heart" or "Jeffision" ... the then 45 degrees of my small mind and world. I could now see the full 360 degrees that God had intended and enlightened in my life.

I continued to Pray, Fast, study scripture about loving one another and marriage, praying circles around Shawn and our marriage while reading about how to understand prayer. I continued to seek a greater understanding of marriage while going to David, a new Christian friend and marriage counselor that Shawn and I saw for the previous year and some odd months leading up to our separation. When we had met with him before, none of his previous attempts could help our marriage work. Only Shawn was understanding and attempting to save our marriage. At the same time, I continued to use what he was saying as ammunition to change her or fire back at Shawn because she was in the wrong.

As Yehuda Berg states, "Words are singularly the most powerful force available to humanity. We can choose to use this force constructively with words of encouragement or destructively using words of despair. Words have the energy and power with the ability to help, to heal, to

> **Words kill, words give life; they're either poison or fruit— you choose.**
>
> Matthew 4:4

hinder, to harm, to humiliate, and to humble."

I obviously chose to use them destructively, to hinder, humiliate, and harm Shawn and our marriage. I honestly never realized how painful and powerful these words were to dissolve our union and belittle Shawn. I saw them as just words I said and didn't always mean what I was saying, but there were also a few times when I knew exactly what I was doing and used them like the double-edged sword that I intended. But, those were in the past, and now we could move forward as God intended.

Still, Shawn was very reluctant, and she limited talking to me for months. She would not even want to see me other than one time to come and get more clothes for work. She only took very few personal items in the haste of leaving the house that rainy night and a few more when she stopped by a few days later. When she came to the house, the first thing she said was that she wasn't there to talk, just to get her things and leave. To which I, for the first time in our marriage, concurred with her wishes and will. Although she did tell me that day that I looked good and that she was grateful to God and happy for me that He healed my back.

I continued to remain faithful to God's plan for my life and only concentrating on my daily walk with Him. I started a job making and installing granite countertops since it was a job, even though it was outside my profession in occupational therapy. But it was a job that I was very thankful for, just to get some money flowing as my long term disability pay was ending soon. We had so many new medical bills and had many other bills to try to catch up on since I was only receiving 60 percent of my regular pay while out of work. Thank God, though, for this blessing to help us sustain our basic needs through this trying time in our lives.

I could not return to my previous job, even though I wanted to. They would have loved to have me back, but they had to hire someone else to replace me since my FMLA was only good for one year, and I was gone for almost 1½ years. So I worked long hours making and installing granite. I prayed, prayed and fasted, prayed circles around our marriage, rebuked the devil, generational chains, and the shackles of our past to be removed from our lives.

I continued to pray audaciously and undoubtedly that our marriage's covenant would be rekindled, restored, renewed, refurbished, and refreshed. I prayed that it would flourish prosperously and in accordance with His perfect will and His perfect way. I also committed that I would wake up every morning and don the armor of God to protect Shawn, our family, and the covenant of our marriage forever until death do us part as He intended from the beginning.

One day I heard about an upcoming conference on marriage from a radio program. I prayed that if I stepped out in faith and bought these tickets in honor of God and our marriage, Shawn would agree to attend. So I bought the tickets and prayed over them every day. I slowly continued to pick up PRN (as needed) jobs in Occupational Therapy as they became available and eventually landed my current full-time position as an Occupational Therapy Assistant in Sandusky, Ohio. When I applied for this job, I would drive past the building daily on my way to and from my PRN jobs in the area and pray that if it was part of God's plan for me/our lives, it would be done in His name.

We continued to stay married but were still separated and continued to concentrate on our healing individually. Through Christian counseling with our CNC Pastor Troy and/or David, the marriage counselor, we focused our efforts on growing our individual relationships with God as a top priority. We understood that there could not be an us until we knew who we were individually and that our relationship with God was solid. We understood that He was the One that first loved us and that He is the One we should love first.

This would eventually allow us to love each other again, even though neither of us expressed this to the other at that time. And we did not know that the other was seeking counsel with David at the same time.

The week of the "A Marriage Worth Fighting For" conference came and I asked Shawn to attend. She quickly and abruptly responded, "No!" But that was okay to me because I already knew that if it was part of the plans that God had for us, it would come to fruition. I just continued to pray and asked other mutual Christian friends near and far to pray that Shawn would be open to attending and change her mind. Two days before the conference, Shawn asked about the conference and who the guest speaker was. It was the amazing Kirk Cameron.

She said that she would go, but only because she didn't want our money to go to waste and because it was a possible once in a lifetime chance to see/meet him. We attended the conference and heard an amazing depiction and assessment of our very lives. At the end of the conference, Kirk asked if he had explicitly touched anyone's lives in a moment of prayer over all marriages. We both raised our hands, and he then asked all couples personally having difficulties in their marriages to please come forward.

He then had the approximately 15 couples kneel and prayed a special prayer over each of our struggling marriages. With both of us in tears and holding hands, humbly bowed, and our marriage being prayed over in the presence of God, I felt a definitive shift in Shawn's presence at that very moment. After we stood and wiped our tears, Shawn's demeanor and body language changed toward me while visiting with some CNC friends attending the conference and happened to be in the front row.

You see, God already knew that we were going to need individual and couple support from another Godly couple from our CNC family and our past. They expressed their love toward us, not knowing about all of the storms we had endured or being currently separated and saying how good I looked after being healed. Shawn seemed so different toward me during dinner and the one-hour drive home.

I continued to give all of the praise and thanks to God that He was moving in our marriage again. The fact of the matter was that he never stopped.

Another couple of days after this conference, Shawn decided after almost two months of separation to go out on another dinner date with me. It felt like she was giving me a test, but there was no way I could fail because it was all God that was in me answering each and every question. When we left the restaurant, we ran into another couple we didn't know who were sitting on a bench outside. We each said "Hello" to the other and then he referenced their love for God and asked if we were Christians. He stated how his wife was saved from a tremendous battle of illness with her heart and had literally died. And he talked about the Grace of God.

I told them of my healing and how God's Grace healed my heart and my spirit and body. He said that he was a prophet of God and that he had a message for us, as well. He said that he could see that we had been through some tremendous trials, but he saw us as a couple in the future and said that he could see "Healing Waters." And in the days following, Shawn decided to come home and give us another chance by the Grace of God.

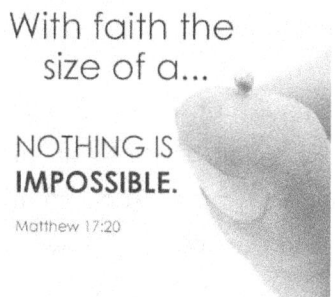

Through all of these trials, I myself have learned that the power of audacious and undoubtable Prayer, Obedience, and Faith is enough to withstand any storm no matter what it may look like in the flesh. I have also learned that staying in prayer daily is far easier to withstand the everyday grind of life.

Recently I have read that during a hurricane — one of the worst types of storms in the sea or land — the fish that are out at sea, or those that go out to sea when the storms come, always have a better chance of survival. They can go deeper in the water and avoid the turbulent waters above by avoiding the waves' circulation during the violent storms. You see, the deeper they go, the less violent the circulation of the storm becomes, and there is a much smaller threat to their overall well-being. And if they go deep enough, there is no increased threat to them at all.

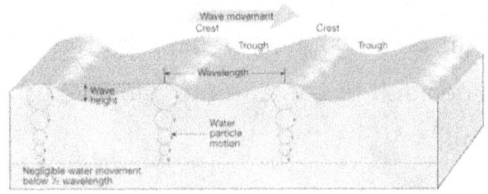

Simplified schematic showing the parts of an ocean wave. At the surface,

I believe this to be true with Christians as well in regards to our lives and in our daily walk with God. Storms will come and go, but it is how we perceive and apply the Word of God to our lives when there are no storms, and when the storms come. "When I'm worried, it's usually because I'm trying to do everything myself. When I'm at peace, it's usually because I remember that God is in control" (Dave Willis).

The deeper we go into His Living Word and remain in His presence each day by prayer and supplication, the less likely the world's effect and the storms will have on our daily lives. So, leave it to God, and our minds will be much more clear to the path He has chosen for us to walk. And the less likely we will be personally affected when adversity arises in our lives. There will be fewer adverse effects on our marriages. *"For I know the plans I have for you, declares the Lord, "plans to prosper you and not to harm you, plans to give you hope and a future"* (Jeremiah 29:11 NIV).

And together, you will be protected and more balanced to be able to adjust and withstand and/or assist others as a light in their storms. We are meant to be a lighthouse of God's Love and Light. But we can only be that vessel if we are plugged into Him! He is the source, *"The way, the Truth and the Life" (John 14:6 NKJV).* When we are in His presence and reading His word, "It is far easier to understand His plan for our lives and give counsel when asked if we always have a ready word" (Glen Ball).

Shawn and I are continuously praying, learning, and leaning on God for insight, understanding, wisdom, and discernment from the Holy Spirit. This helps us assist our adult children and the generations to come with similar circumstances or situations as they may arise in their lives. We can give insight into previous issues that we have dealt with in our own marriage. We seek to be an example of His love, life, and light each and every day. Life and its trials are a learning process, but it's much easier when you know the fight is already won. Thank You, Jesus!

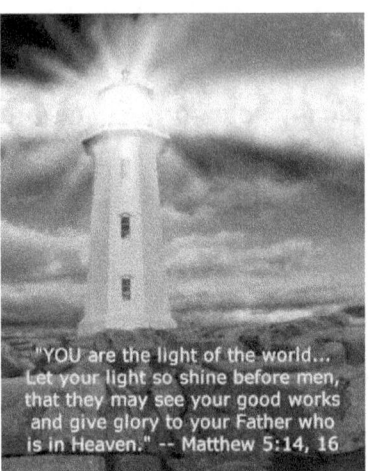

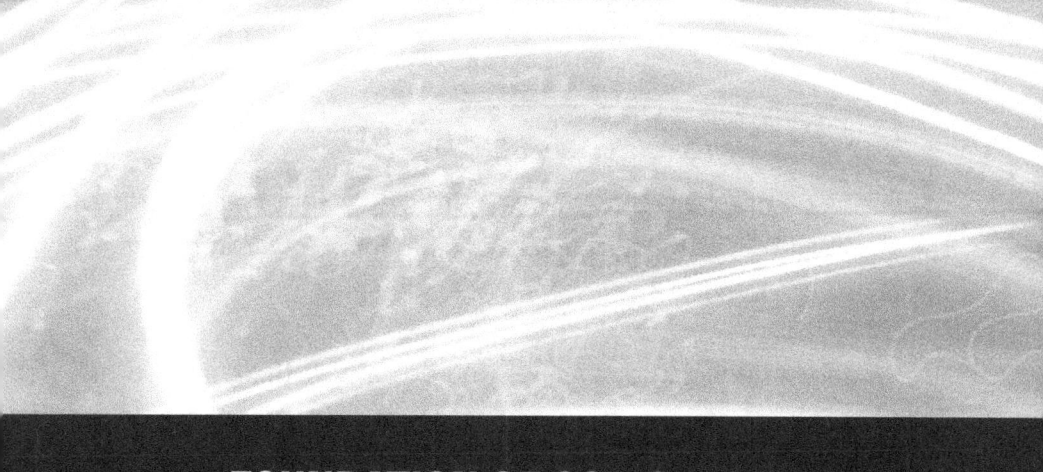

FOUNDATION OF GOD'S WORD AND IN YOUR MARRIAGE

We continued to seek counsel and continued to make God the priority in our lives and upon our marriage through Faith, Obedience, and Prayer. We both now understand that during these difficult seasons and storms in our lives, it was the continual, audacious, and undoubtable prayer to right our lives that actually saved us and our marriage. Our love for Him is what allowed us to remain together by His Grace, just like when the Israelites marched circles around Jericho and prayed for the walls to fall. The wall in front of my eyes, around Shawn's heart, and the despair on and over our marriage finally fell.

It has honestly taken several months to almost a year to get to where we currently are in our marriage today — a lot of old bridges needed to be crossed or rebuilt. With the communication barriers opened to establish a new understanding from God's Word in our marriage, old thoughts have been diminished, shackles removed, and the elimination of walking on eggshells is now gone. With Shawn not being fearful of the past "Me" or not being able to speak her mind freely, our marriage has been able to flourish.

But when God does a good thing, He does a new thing in all of us. There have been many conversations that have occurred that needed to happen years prior.

Life is so much easier with having these new and open lines of communication, and a true understanding of God's love for us and our marriage. We have managed to eliminate ill feelings, embrace fresh beginnings, and commit to a future of Agape Love, Mutual Respect, Admiration, and Sacrifice. It honestly wasn't easy at first, as all marriages have their daily challenges. Still, we had to establish the idea of Grace and apply this mentality in our marriage and toward one another.

Grace — "the love and mercy are given to us by God because God desires us to have it, not necessarily because of anything we have done to earn it." It is not a created substance of any kind. "Grace is favor, the free and undeserved help that God gives us to respond to his call to become children of God, adoptive sons, partakers of the divine nature and of eternal life." Christians understand it to be a spontaneous gift from God to people, "generous, free and totally unexpected and undeserved." It takes the form of divine favor, love, clemency, and a share in the divine life of God.

Also contributing to our marriage's growth is that we have since learned and apply all of the principles of a successful marriage through our version of the house building principle. We feel it is a must for all marriages.

First, building on God's rock solid and living word is a must. This principle is the understanding and application of His Living Word. We read the Bible, other encouragement resources and pray together every morning, throughout our day, and at night when we go to bed. We pray together in agreement for specific situations, circumstances, all marriages, other individuals, and we take turns praying at all times. And we believe that this is a very crucial and important point, to pray as one body in Christ's name together and alternating praying aloud to put what is being prayed into the atmosphere and over the spiritual realm.

A foundation built on the solid ground remains stable to withstand the rains, floods, and wind when they come (see Matthew 7:24-27). Here is a simple prayer that you may choose, which was given to me by my Grandmother, Annabel Lind, many years ago. Her and my Papa, Jacob Lind Jr., use to pray together every morning.

Good Morning God!

You are ushering in another day,
Untouched and freshly new.
So here I am to ask you, God,
If You'll renew me too.

*Forgive the many errors that I made
yesterday, and let me try again, Dear God
to walk closer in Your way.*

*But Lord, I am well aware,
I can't make it on my own.
So take my hand and hold it tight,
for I cannot walk alone.*

— *Unknown*

The second principle is to build a foundation in your marriage through mutual respect for one another. We now show mutual respect for one another and communicate daily about all aspects of our day. We are made equally in the image of God and choose to use Philippians 2:2

as our main resource. *"Then make me truly happy by agreeing wholeheartedly with each other, loving one another, and working together with one mind and purpose."*

God intended us to be one with Him and each other from the day that we agreed in His name to receive the Covenant of Marriage. However this, though, requires a lot of self discipline and is not always easy to do. But through Grace, it can be accomplished. Some of the mutual respect attributes include our tone, words, eye contact, body language, not assuming, listening, and not interrupting one another. These are all conscientious choices that will affect each conversation and every type of situation or circumstance that you will endure as a married couple.

Tone — The choice we make in how we say things is a key factor in the way all perceive and the way information is received. Ninety percent of friction in daily life is caused by the wrong tone of our voice. "Let your gentleness be evident to all" (Philippians 4:5 NIV).

Words — The words that we choose each day make all of the difference in the world. If we speak kind words over or in someone's life, we too will probably receive kindness and grace in return. If we speak angered, disrespectful, and demeaning words, we will create strife and receive in return, anger, frustration, and/or grief. *"Words kill, words give life; they're either poison or fruit" (Matthew 4:4 NIV).*

Eye contact — If we are not looking at our spouse when they are talking or continually looking away, we are not giving them the sense that we care about what they are saying, or that other things around us are more important. *"Light in a messenger's eyes brings joy to the heart, and good news gives health to the bones"* (Proverbs 15:30 NIV).

Body Language — The way you stand, sit, turn away, and place your hands on your hips or head states far more what you think than what is being said or received. *"A happy heart makes the face cheerful, but heartache crushes the spirit"* (Proverbs 15:13 NIV).

Not Assuming — You know the old adage for the word ass/u/me being broken down. *"Fools find no pleasure in understanding, but delight in airing their own opinions"* (Proverbs 18:2 NIV).

Listening — No one likes to be talking about something of interest or that needs to be communicated and have another person say, "What did you say?" because they were not paying attention. "The biggest communication problem is we don't listen to understand, we listen to reply" (Unknown). *"A fool takes no pleasure in understanding, but only in expressing his opinion"* (Proverbs 18:2 NIV).

Interruption — I personally do not know anyone who likes to be interrupted or not having their chance to communicate. Guys, this is a key element when she's at her wit's end, and we're watching a ball game. You might want to just turn that television off and cover yourself on two or three of these foundations. All of these offenses are basically saying you're not worth my time. *"Even a fool who keeps silent is considered wise; when he closes his lips, he is deemed intelligent"* (Proverbs 17:28 NIV).

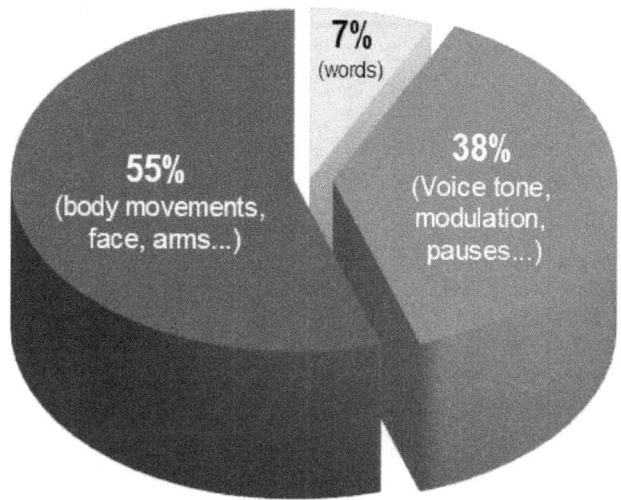

Key Elements of Successful Communication, Albert Mehrabian

If you find yourself at the short end of any of these situations, you are not a failure or have not failed your marriage. It takes a lot of patience, time, and effort to put these principles into practice. This is also where two things need to occur. The first is asking for Grace from God, and the second is for your spouse to provide grace to you. Ask God for forgiveness, and He will grant you Grace because He loves you. Jesus said in Matthew 7:7, *"Ask, and it will be given to you: seek, and you will find: knock, and it will be opened to you."*

This leads us to the next step, which is the main floor of the house principle. The subfloor is where you personally need to accept Responsibility for your choices, actions, feelings, needs, and blame. We are all responsible for how we act, react, choices we make, what we say, and who we blame for each and every circumstance that we will endure in our life and marriage.

"Let no man say when he is tempted, I am tempted of God; for God cannot be tempted with evil, neither tempteth he any man. But every man is tempted, when he is drawn away of his own lust, and enticed" (James 1:13-14 KJV).

"For every man shall bear his own burden" (Galatians 6:5).

There are two key principles to this phase, and they are in the words "I — which accepts responsibility" and "You — which points blame on another," namely your spouse. The first is, but the second is not donning the whole Armor of God, which is to protect and serve each other with truth, righteousness, peace, and faith. Nor allowing for Salvation or being in the Spirit, which is the Word of God.

Continuing with the house building principle, your house needs to be built on the cornerstones to build the main upright structure. I like using the word cornerstone as it was used in the Old Testament because it speaks of soundness. That is what you want your whole house (and marriage) to be built upon — sound principle and structurally sound. Seven different times in the Bible, God mentions the cornerstone in the Old Testament. The following verses give reference: *Isaiah 28:16, Psalm 118:22, 1 Peter 2:6, Acts 4:11, 1 Peter 2:7, Ephesians 2:19-22, and 1 Peter 2:5-6.*

The cornerstones are of key importance, as are the four primary principles to the structure of your marriage. These four cornerstones are as follows, but in no particular order as they are all important — Wisdom, Honesty, Empathy, and Blessing.

Wisdom — Having insight with certain situations or circumstances, and/or having knowledge and understanding based on sound judgments or being wise to previous matters experienced. *"If any of you lacks wisdom, you should ask God, who gives generously to all without finding fault, and it will be given to you" (James 1:5 NIV).*

Honesty — Being upright or forthcoming and having the quality of honor and integrity in all situations and circumstances no matter the outcome or consequence. *"Good judgment wins favor, but the way of the unfaithful leads to their destruction. All who are prudent act with knowledge, but fools expose their folly" (Proverbs 13:15-16 NIV).*

Empathy — This is putting yourself in someone else's shoes to attempt to vicariously understand what they are going through or feeling during difficult circumstances or situations. *"Rejoice with those who rejoice; mourn with those who mourn. Live in harmony with one another. Do not be proud, but be willing to associate with people of low position. Do not be conceited" (Romans 12:15-16 NIV).*

Blessing — Giving grace and mercy that you would save for yourself and doing it graciously, lovingly, and happily to all in need to show God's love, light, and life coming through you. *"Finally, all of you, be like-minded, be sympathetic, love one another, be compassionate and humble. Do not repay evil with evil or insult with insult. On the contrary, repay evil with blessing, because to this you were called so that you may inherit a blessing" (1 Peter 3:8-9 NIV).*

Your structure also needs a doorway to lead you in and out, through the ebbs and flows of the Covenant of marriage. This passageway is known as Service, which is helping one another and is devoted to a particular positive outcome or benefit. It is a place to create a safe haven to protect or block out against the unknown or create a secure refuge.

"Whoever dwells in the shelter of the Most High will rest in the shadow of the Almighty. I will say to the Lord, 'He is my refuge and my fortress, my God, in whom I trust.' Surely he will save you from the fowler's snare and from the deadly pestilence. He will cover you with his feathers, and under his wings, you will find refuge; his faithfulness will be your shield and rampart. You will not fear the terror of night, nor the arrow that flies by day, nor the pestilence that stalks in the darkness, nor the plague that destroys at midday. A thousand may fall at your side, ten thousand at your right hand, but it will not come near you. You will only observe with your eyes and see the punishment of the wicked. If you say, 'The Lord is my refuge,' and you make the Most High your dwelling, no harm will overtake you. No disaster will come near your tent. For he will command his angels concerning you to guard you in all your ways; they will lift you up in their hands, so that you will not strike your foot against a stone. You will tread on the lion and the cobra; you will trample the great lion and the serpent. 'Because he loves me,' says the Lord, 'I will rescue him; I will protect him, for he acknowledges my name. He will call on me, and I will answer him; I will be with him in trouble, I will deliver him and honor him. With long life I

will satisfy him and show him my salvation'" (Psalm 91, NIV).

You are also to assist one another in the daily grind of life. It is not for one person to take care of all the daily chores such as cooking, cleaning, finances, child care, and other responsibilities. You were given a partner to walk through the daily tasks of life as Helpers to one another. God gave Adam a helper by creating Eve. *"And the Lord God said, 'It is not good that man should be alone: I will make him a helper comparable to him'" (Genesis 2:18 NKJV).*

And another key point to this is the word "comparable." You see, God gave us a helpmate that is deemed equal to us so that we can work together in His name. He is the only one greater. He expects us to treat one another with mutual respect, dignity, honor, grace, mercy, and love. We should happily provide these services to one another to walk through the daily ebbs and flows of life in unity.

Side note — There should also be one more important application of this message. And this needs to be applied to your hearts daily, Joshua 24:15: *"As for me and my house, we will serve the Lord."* This must be applied to your marriage and life daily by serving Our Lord God with ALL your heart, soul, and mind!

Serving God every day will let you understand that you are being held accountable for everything you do, say, and are ... and whether your actions are acceptable and pleasing to God, not one another. This will allow you to know that you are servicing your spouse as He has intended for you.

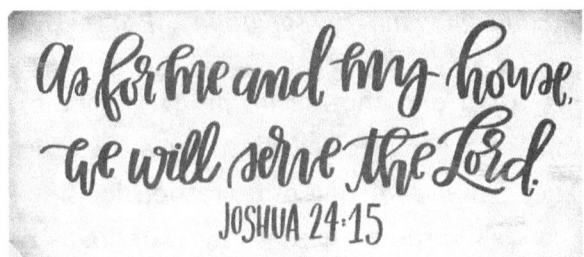

Another major structural component of the house principle is the roof or covering. Love covers, protects, heals, supports, strengthens, and provides faith. We need to complete this covering over our marriages each day with Prayer and Love, knowing that you have each other's back no matter the circumstance or situation. Unconditionally — without limitations or conditions. You should know that you have your spouse' and your spouse will always have your "6" in good times and bad, through sickness and through health, for richer or for poorer, to comfort and console, to laugh with you and to cry by your side. *"Above all, love each other deeply, because love covers over a multitude of sins" (1 Peter 4:8, NIV).*

With this being said, unconditional love does not mean unconditional acceptance of bad behavior or poor choices as I had previously committed in my life and in our marriage.

There should also be a chimney as a necessity of the house. This is to allow for the bad days and negative innuendoes of the past to be disbursed from your lives, never to be brought back into your home or lives again. Let go of the war stories, judging or keeping score, and give each other the benefit of Grace. We all have bad moments and bad days, so allow these things to be released and dispersed, just like when you throw something into the fireplace. They are incinerated to never be brought back and then dispersed into the environment, never to be collected again.

Once you can release the shackles, chains, and bondage of the negative circumstance or situation, you can overcome a similar situations negative effect because you know that there are no residual feelings associated with this similar situation.

There are issues from everyone's past that we can all harbor or reserve for a later time, be used to demean, or as ammo in the next round. But if we allow this to be the case, it will only fester and cause increased irritation over time. If you have a sore and it continues to be picked at, it will never heal.

The old saying is, "Time heals all wounds." I agree with this statement, but it needs a little something, and that something is called Grace. Grace allows for healing and forgiveness. It also provides for those bad days or when one of you makes a mistake.

So, if you're going to start a fire, start it with the logs of Grace in the fireplace and choose to let it go and let God. Jesus said in Matthew 7:3, *"And why do you look at the speck in your brother's eye, but do not consider the plank in your own eye"* (NKJV).

Lastly, you need an insurance policy to cover your marriage covenant, and this is through Faith. *"Now Faith is the substance of things hoped for, the evidence of things not seen"* (Hebrews 11:1 KJV). Without Faith, what do you really have? Sure, you can be "in Love," but can this withstand all of the trials of Life? You can be with the "man or woman of your dreams." But looks fade away, and love based on Phileo feelings will change with circumstances and over time.

And of course, you can put your faith in financial security and health policies. But this is another topic that no one can guarantee, I am living proof of that. There are no guarantees in life, and there will always be situations and circumstances that will arise. But through Faith in Our Lord and Savior, Jesus Christ, days are a lot less stressful when you know that you are covered by His Blood.

"Do not be anxious about anything, but in every situation, by prayer and petition, with thanksgiving, present your requests to God. And the peace of God, which transcends all understanding, will guard your hearts and your minds in Christ Jesus" (Philippians 4:6-7 NIV).

And with similar application of these house building principles, you too can live a healthier, more stable lifestyle in the Name of God. His Agape Love is never-ending and never-failing. And because of His unconditional Love, you, too, can experience Agape love provided from you to your husband or your wife that will last a lifetime because it only comes from God.

ETERNALLY AND HAPPILY MARRIED FOREVER AFTER

Now in our 18th year of marriage, I can say that we are definitively on the right road. We are undoubtedly honoring the Covenant of Our Marriage as God intended for it to be from the beginning. But it is by Eternal Grace and the gift from God that Our marriage has survived all of the physical, emotional, financial, and ethical storms and Spiritual warfare. We can finally say that we love each other because we Love God First!

And others say that this is apparent in our interactions with one another and other couples, as well. We have an Agape love from God, and for one another allowing us to live with Grace, Mercy, Peace, Respect, and Understanding each and every day. We were just asked a few days ago if we were Newlyweds. I guess the waitress that asked must have seen our T-shirts that said, "Born to Love," and saw God's light and love shining through us. We are still involved in the couples ministry at CNC and are the facilitators of an affiliated Facebook page called "Marriage Matters" through CNC, and now "TYING KNOTS" on Facebook which is a daily blog associated to this book. We try to give inspiration, support, and Love to all other couples as God and Pastor Tina intended for us to do from the beginning.

We also continue to attend a special conference, "Marriage for Life," every February in Amish Country, Ohio. It's very dear to us and has now expanded to two weekends in January and February. It allows us to further our Covenant commitment with other like-minded couples. We have found many different couples at this conference interested in seeing marriages receive inspiration, survive, and thrive with Beau and friends' help. We understand that there are many marriages out there that are or were very similar to ours in dysfunction, despair, and unknown circumstances. So it always helps to surround yourself and support others going through similar situations and just be around like-minded Godly couples to give you strength, hope, and comfort.

And the absolute best message that I/WE can continue to provide to you is as follows. NEVER GIVE UP and CONTINUE TO PRAY specifically over your spouse for whatever their greatest needs are in agreement with God. Pray audaciously and undoubtedly because God has you covered but you need to step out in Faith showing that you Trust Him and that you place "ALL CONTROL" in His hands. Release all control over to Him, allowing Him to do His perfect will and His perfect way to, over, in, with, through, and upon your lives as He sees fit. Asking God to show you how to better your personal walk with Him and grow your relationship to Love Him more with all your heart, mind, soul, and spirit.

I/We honestly believe that we were only able to accomplish this as we grew our personal and spiritual relationship to be in one accord with Him before we could actually be as one with each other. Just like the concept of the three strand cord. *"And the two shall become one flesh; so then they are no longer two, but one flesh" (Mark 10:8 NKJV).*

Ecclesiastes 4:9-12 (KJV) says, "Two are better than one, because they have a good reward for their labor. For if they fall, the one will lift up his mate, but woe to him that is alone when he falls: for he has not another to help him up. Again, if two lie together, then they have heat: but how can one be warm alone? And if one prevails against him, two shall withstand him; and a threefold cord is not quickly broken."

One concept that I/we failed to understand all of these prior years is that God was actually giving each of us a helper, confidant, friend, and lover. He had given us a partner to increase understanding and a special person to share ideas and assist one another rather than rely only on ourselves and our own understanding.

Shawn was a confident young woman who worked hard and didn't need anyone's help to care for her, or care for and help raise her child when we first met. And I was a man that could get anything accomplished and wasn't afraid to take the world by storm. But what we failed to understand was that two are better than one, especially if you are working in the same direction, with the same Faith, determination, in accordance with the Will of God.

I/We know that if Shawn and I had understood this concept from the beginning of our marriage, we would have started off on the right foot. We would have known that God needs to be the center of ALL marriages and all things related to your marriage. His Word is the center strand, and we just needed to wrap ourselves around Him becoming one. We believe that when you accept the Covenant of Marriage by His Grace, you literally need to tie a knot in that three-strand cord, so you have something to hang on to.

Recall a definitive remembrance of why you got married and who you are really being held accountable to. And each time the two of you make a new commitment to God in your marriage, tie another knot. It becomes a climbing rope with several knots to figuratively and literally stand on as you and your spouse go through the trials of everyday life and through your marriage.

These new commitments can be anything that shares God's love, life, and light toward God, each other, and/or to this world. It will bring the two of you closer to Him and ultimately one another. Some examples of this would be: one or both of you giving your life over to God.

When one of you makes a choice to change for the betterment of your relationship by spending more time together rather than isolating yourself with friends, sports, or other interests that limit quality time together, good things can happen. You could overcome a life trial, such as paying off a major purchase or paying off a long-term debt obligation. Or it could be something as simple as a little ongoing post that we share weekly on social media called, "Where are the Linds?" People guess where we currently are in God's beautiful world based solely on pictures.

We also host and greet at our home church (CNC — Lorain), spreading God's love and meeting new couples while wearing a shirt that says, "Born to Love." And we serve in other capacities within CNC as well, such as the heading of the Communion ministry. We also like to make a point of randomly contacting other couples to go out to dinner and other events. Sometimes taking dinner to them at their home to share Gods' love for them. As I previously mentioned, "Marriage Matters" is the CNC couples Ministry as well. These are a few small examples to make a loving and lasting impact on another couple's life and share God's Love with Everyone. We are here to "Love One Another" and "Celebrate Gods Love" with all.

Thanks, Pastors Louis and Tina Kayatin, for assisting in instilling God's love in us and others! So, I highly recommend finding a Home church like CNC to get planted so you can grow and flourish in new and exciting relationships. "TYING KNOTS" with other Godly couples in your own community as well as all over the world.

A LITTLE EXTRA LOVE

from Jeff & Shawn

Live Right!

Help one another by always having your spouse's back, whether it be with household chores to lighten the load of a stressful day or to just allow for him/her to know without a doubt that you're willing to be there. Be their confidant, their support, and/or to just speak one of their love languages. There is no better way to make your spouse feel at ease or appreciated than by helping cook a meal or setting the table while they are cooking. And a slow dance in the kitchen is highly recommended while the food is cooking. You never know, maybe a little romance might get a little something else cooking later! That's a plug for you guys out there needing a little incentive to give this a try!

Shawn and I take turns for the most part by communicating each day or the night before who will be cooking that night and what we are having. We have already planned ahead for the week on what food we have at our house.

Sometimes things change in a flash, and then it takes one of you stepping up on the other's behalf if there has been a bad, stressful, or tiring day. Sometimes to hear the words, "Hey honey, I got the meal tonight, so you can just take a break and relax," mean everything. Or sometimes it just means, by living modestly, you can afford to make it a dinner out for some alone time for the two of you. This makes life stressors fade away and you can reconnect with your spouse rather than cooking that night.

Make ALL financial decisions together and discuss all major purchases that are over an agreed-upon limit with each other before making the purchase. Another helpful tip is to not make any significant purchases for at least 40 days. This allows for the "I think I have to have it" or "I want it" mentality to wear off. Furthermore, the significance of 40 days is important as well, with this being the standard in several situations throughout the Bible. It happened with Elijah, Moses, Jesus, Noah, and several others. It also speaks of a "waiting period" or "fasting period" of 40 days.

Living modestly has to be a significant standard in your lives. By living modestly, you can get yourself out of debt. We continue to do this each and every day, allowing us to be able to pay off medical bills, pay back family members that have assisted us financially along our journey, help others as we can, and relieve everyday stressors that use to weigh us down tremendously causing increased issues between us. We can pay it forward as aforementioned with dinners by assisting others in need like providing a Thanksgiving meal to a family in need each year. It allows for unexpected car repairs, and of course, giving our Tithe regularly, which enables our home church to thrive and assist others in need.

Lastly, be thankful for Everything, and in Everything, give Thanks. *"In everything give thanks: for this is the will of God in Christ Jesus concerning you" (1 Thessalonians 5:18, KJV).* Giving thanks for even the small things in your life leads to contentment in life and marriage. Being content and thankful allows you to grow and mature Spiritually as well. You can have a greater relationship with God, which, in turn enables you to have a more excellent relationship with everyone.

Love One Another!

God just wants us to love one another as He loves us. It's really not hard at all to be a shining example of God's love by making lasting relationships with other Godly and like-minded Christian couples — others who are looking to make their marriage a priority. Like you are doing with yours.

Philippians 2:1-4 states, "Therefore if there is any consolation in Christ, if any comfort of love, if any fellowship of the Spirit, if any affection and mercy, fulfill my joy by being like-minded, having the same love, being of one accord, of one mind. Let nothing be done through selfish ambition and conceit, but in lowliness of mind let each esteem others better than himself. Let each of you look out not only for his own interests, but for the interests of others" (NKJV).

Love others, and this will allow God's love, life, and light to shine through you to all of the world. Other couples are looking for you as a God-fearing couple to be an inspiration or example of steadfast love throughout trials. You can be steadfast or be there as a confidant in a world of change. This allows all other couples to feel loved even though you may be going through trials yourselves.

We still continue to deal with some of our past situations that just didn't go away because of my many bad choices and mistakes. But we continue to allow God's light to shine through us, just like I said in Chapter 3. I wanted Our marriage and life to be like those other God-fearing couples that I saw and encountered week after week at CNC. Just love one another and show everyone the same kindness, love, respect, and honor that you would like to be shown in every situation throughout life.

"Believers Are Salt and Light"

In The Beatitudes, Jesus went up on the mountain after seeing the multitudes to teach His disciples:

"You are the salt of the earth; but if the salt loses its flavor, how shall it be seasoned? It is good for nothing but to be thrown out and trampled underfoot by men."

"You are the light of the world. A city that is set on a hill cannot be hidden. Nor do they light a lamp and put it under a basket, but on a lampstand, and it gives light to all who are in the house. Let your light shine before men, that they may see your good works and glorify your Father in Heaven" (Matthew 5: 13-16, NKJV).

Pray Hard!

This, by far, is the most essential part of anything that I/we can offer your marriage. Pray audaciously and undoubtedly. Pray for God's will and way to be done so that you can come into agreement with whatever He has in store for you. It may not always look like what you want it to look like, but trust in Him. You will obviously be better off in the end.

God has not answered several of my prayers that I thought were best for me and my circumstances. But in the end, as always, my life has become better than I could have ever imagined. And some prayers, I'm/We're patiently waiting for answers to this very day. But I/we continue to pray to come into agreement for these people and these situations each day.

Your prayers should be as if your life depends on them also. Even if you are praying on another's behalf, again, you need to pray as if it means the world to you, as well. Even if you are not invested in the situation. Pray for peace and clarity in every situation and for Grace to be the final outcome for all involved.

Pray over your marriage daily. Pray that God gives you wisdom, truth, understanding, peace, and love throughout each day. Pray that God allows you to be the best "You" that you can be each and every day toward Him, your spouse, your children, your parents, your job, etc. And Pray that God fulfills all of your spouse's greatest needs each day, which will allow them to be the best they can be each and every day as well. This makes your relationship even better when they are being who God wants them to be too.

"So Jesus answered them and said to them, 'Assuredly, I say to you, if you have faith and do not doubt, you will not only do what was done to the fig tree, but also if you say to this mountain, Be removed and be cast into the sea, it will be done. And whatever things you ask in prayer, believing, you will receive'" (Matthew 21:21-22, NKJV).

Father God, Shawn and I agree this very moment for all marriages, especially those in need of a breakthrough, a special touch, a message of hope, or to have Faith even if it's the size of a mustard seed. We ask that you touch each of these marriages, Father God, as you did ours with a sense of Hope, Grace, Peace, and Mercy. This releases your presence to intercede on their behalf and to reflect Your Love, Heavenly Father. We agree for marriages to turn toward You because You are the only source that they need to be restored, renewed, rekindled, reestablished, and reborn in this very moment. We agree with other godly men and women, Father God, praying for ALL marriages to withstand the Prince of Darkness's temptations and the storms revolving around them. We ask that you are their shelter and their refuge, providing peace, calmness, and a sense of security like they are in the eye of a storm. We ask that you give them the strength to relinquish everything over to You, letting go of all control this very moment. This surrender allows You to move on their behalf and to turn stony hearts into fleshy hearts. This allows the chains, shackles, and bondage of past generational curses and past mistakes to be forgiven by Your Grace, Love, and Presence, in Jesus' Mighty and Glorious Name.

Amen, Amen, and Amen.

Afterword

To accomplish this kind of Marriage, it will take great effort on your and your spouse's part. Still, it will be well worth the experience when you take the time to apply these principles toward your relationship with Our Heavenly Father's guidance. Then, continue to nurture, care, and feed the seed you planted in your marriage and watch it root, sprout, grow, and flourish into a full-fledged Oak tree.

Dating &
Engagement
2000

Wedding Day
August 24, 2002

Our Happy New Family

Our Covenant Began

Honeymoon

Vacation Jamaica

Vacation Talla Race Track

Cancun

Bahamas

My "trophy wife" and I at our annual company's drunken bash

Inside the "mansion"

My recliner and window view

The so-called "mansion"

Our adult children and us

We are very proud of our adult children

Our new chapter of life as Grandparents

One of many "Marriage for Life" conferences

Hosting at CNC

Fall at CNC

Recent pic of my friend, Rapheal

The beginning of "Couples Connecting" gatherings with our great friends, Marty & Eydie.

Christmas 2018

Easter 2019

Summer 2019

Various pictures of
"Where are the Lind's?"
in God's amazing world!

Continuing the trend "Where are the Lind's locally around Northeast Ohio and from afar for our oldest son and daughter by Love's destination Wedding in Oahu, Hawaii.

The Love Chapter

If I speak with the tongues of men and of angels, but
have not love, I am a noisy gong or a clanging cymbal.
And if I have prophetic powers and understand all mysteries
and all knowledge, and if I have all faith, so as to remove
mountains, but have not love, I am nothing. If I give away all
I have, and if I deliver my body to be burned,
but have not love, I gain nothing.

Love is patient and kind; love is not jealous or boastful;
it is not arrogant or rude. Love does not insist on
its own way; it is not irritable or resentful; it does not
rejoice at wrong, but rejoices in the right.
Love bears all things, believes all things, hopes all things,
endures all things. Love never ends. As for prophecies, they
will pass away; as for tongues, they will cease, as for knowledge,
it will pass away. For our knowledge is imperfect, and our
prophecy is imperfect; but when the perfect comes,
the imperfect will pass away.

When I was a child, I spoke like a child, I thought like
a child, I reasoned like a child; but when I became a man,
I gave up childish ways. For now we see in a mirror dimly,
but then face to face. Now I know in part; then I shall
understand fully, even as I have been fully understood.
So faith, hope, love abide, these three;
but the greatest of these is love.

I Corinthians 13: 1-13.

www.ingramcontent.com/pod-product-compliance
Lightning Source LLC
Chambersburg PA
CBHW072202100526

44589CB00015B/2337